Winning Strategies *for* Developing Grant Proposals

2nd Edition   Dr. Beverly Browning

Thompson Publishing Group, Inc.
1725 K St. NW, 7th Floor
Washington, DC 20006
202-872-4000 (Editorial Offices)
1-800-677-3789 (Customer Service)

THOMPSON

Insight you trust.

www.thompson.com

î THOMPSON

Thompson Publishing Group, Inc.

Thompson Publishing Group is a trusted name in authoritative analysis of laws, regulations and business practices that helps corporate, government and other professionals develop regulatory compliance strategies. Since 1972, thousands of professionals in business, government, law and academia have relied on Thompson Publishing Group for the most authoritative, timely and practical guidance available.

Thompson offers loose leaf services, books, specialty newsletters, audio conferences and online products in a number of subject and regulatory compliance areas. These Thompson products provide insightful analysis, practical guidance and real-world solutions to the challenges facing grants professionals today and beyond. More information about Thompson's product offerings is available at http://www.thompson.com.

To order any Thompson products or additional copies of this book, please contact us:

Call: 1-800-677-3789
Online: www.thompson.com
Fax: 1-800-999-5661
Email: service@thompson.com
Mail: Thompson Publishing Group
Subscription Service Center
PO Box 26185, Tampa, FL 33623-6185

❦❦❦❦❦❦❦❦❦❦❦❦❦

Associate Publisher: Denise A. Lamoreaux
Senior Managing Editor: Donald B. Hoffman
Desktop Publisher: Laurie S. Clark
Cover design: Ellen Hamilton

Winning Strategies For Developing Grant Proposals (2nd Edition) is published by Thompson Publishing Group, Inc., 1725 K St. N.W., 7th Floor, Washington, DC 20006.

This publication is designed to be accurate and authoritative, but the publisher is not rendering legal, accounting or other professional services. If legal or other expert advice is desired, retain the services of an appropriate professional.

Copyright ©2006 by Thompson Publishing Group, Inc. All rights reserved.

Photocopying without the publisher's consent is strictly prohibited. Consent needs to be granted to reproduce individual items for personal or internal use by the Copyright Clearance Center, 222 Rosewood Drive, Danvers, MA 01923.

Printed in the United States

ISBN 1-930872-82-8

Preface

Competing for federal and private grant dollars has never been more competitive and challenging. Federal spending priorities are always changing, as are the giving priorities of corporate and private grantmakers. State and local governments, colleges and universities, hospitals and community and other nonprofit organizations are all vying for a slice of the more than $400 billion in federal funds awarded annually. Hundreds of millions of dollars in private funding is also offered each year. Grants are awarded to support programs ranging from community health to education to homeland security to transportation to social services. The key to tapping these dollars is knowing where to find them and then, writing a clear, compelling, convincing and authoritative grant proposal.

Today's grants environment has come a long way from the days of hearing about grants by word of mouth or by constantly calling grantmaker offices. There was a time when preparing a grant proposal meant hours of research at a library, scouring directories and reports for clues to where to find grant dollars. And only then did the long process of preparing the paper proposal begin – writing the proposal narrative, compiling a budget, gathering other components and then pulling the whole proposal together to mail to the grantmaker – a task that is still done today, but is waning because of the electronic society in which we now live.

The Web has changed the way we communicate and conduct business. Federal and private grantmakers have rushed to launch e-grants initiatives and processes that have streamlined the way they award grant dollars and how organizations locate and apply for those funds. Grants.gov is the lead portal for searching and applying for federal grants. As of May 2006, Grants.gov had received 45,000 electronic grant applications, a huge leap from the number reported for 2004 (1,000). Private and corporate foundations have also created impressive Web sites that allow grantseekers to search and apply for grant dollars with the click of a mouse. Common grant application forms used by many private grantmakers and other application and proposal forms are available online. The widespread use and acceptance of "e-grants" has made the grantseeking and proposal writing tasks more efficient. But the electronic age has not revised the basic tenets of successful grantseeking – careful, thorough research, efficient financial management and budgeting, and making a persuasive case by demonstrating how your program or meets the grantmaker's funding priorities.

Winning Strategies for Developing Grant Proposals is an authoritative guide to writing effective grant proposals, giving you the edge you need to compete for grant dollars. Written by Dr. Beverly Browning, a leading grantwriting expert, the book analyzes the basic principles of good proposal writing and the latest techniques and strategies for getting your proposals funded. *Winning Strategies* also includes a detailed tutorial of how to register for and get ready to use Grants.gov to apply for federal dollars. Key insights from other grant experts and time-tested tips from grantmakers are also provided in the book.

We are pleased you have purchased *Winning Strategies for Developing Grant Proposals* published by Thompson Publishing Group, the leader in providing cutting-edge information to grants professionals for more than 30 years.

Philip Gabel
President & CEO
Thompson Publishing Group

Gail Vertz
Executive Director
American Association of Grant Professionals

Table of Contents

©Thompson Publishing Group

Introduction

1

To people unfamiliar with the process, grantseeking can be a daunting, even confusing and complex, task. Novices in the grants field often see other organizations receiving grants but fail to understand the process or procedures used to obtain them. It is imperative for organizations seeking funding – whether from federal agencies, private foundations or corporate endowments – to understand the process. Perhaps as equally important is for grantseekers to understand and put into practice effective tools for researching funding sources, defining goals and objectives of proposed projects and activities, and writing sound grant proposals. *Winning Strategies for Developing Grant Proposals* provides those tools for successful grantseeking.

The adage, "the only constant in life is change," applies in the grants environment. While public and private grantmaking has occurred for quite some time, the climate for grantmaking changes constantly. Grantmaking is cyclical and mostly a chameleon of the economy, decade after decade. This means there will be good and bad times to apply for funding, regardless of whether the source is a federal agency, a foundation or a corporation. What does this mean for your organization? It means that you must work aggressively to diversify your external funding streams and that you should never rely on one source of grant funding.

Additionally, the ways and means of researching and applying for grants has changed dramatically in recent years. Once a strictly paper-and-pen project, grantseeking has become an electronic task, as the Web has transformed the way society gathers and exchanges information. Many federal and private grantmaking agencies and corporate giving programs have transformed their grant application mechanisms into streamlined electronic processes. With the click of a mouse, grantseekers can streamline their funding research as well as submit their applications electronically.

Organizations such as yours have been looking for ways to plug the financial leaks in their operating budgets since the beginning of grantmaking. And the demand for your services and programs has always been higher than the amount of internal resources available. To keep doing what your organization does best as a service provider the designated grant writer must always be on the lookout for additional funding. Unless your organization is lucky enough to have a substantial endowment fund or extremely healthy financial reserves, your organization will always be looking for grants and other revenues to meet program needs. That's a constant.

Evolution of Federal Grantmaking

Federal grants-in-aid have been around since the federal government was formed. Over the past two decades, the federal government shifted the responsibility of providing direct program services from federal agencies to state and local agencies. These agencies, in turn, subaward these federal funds to other organizations, such as community action agencies, educational institutions and other nonprofit organizations. With this transfer of direct program management from the federal to state and local levels, many grantseeking agencies found themselves seeking grants from state and local agencies. Total federal funding (grants, cooperative agreements, loans and loan guarantees) topped $400 billion in federal fiscal year 2003, according to a Government Accountability Office report (GAO-05-335). And tied to this funding to states, local governments and nonprofit organizations was a demand for greater accountability for and proper stewardship of public funds.

To ensure greater accountability of federal grant funds and streamline federal grant application and management processes, Congress enacted the Federal Financial Assistance Management Improvement Act of 1999. Commonly called P.L. 106-107, the act's objectives were to improve the effectiveness and performance of federal financial assistance programs, simplify federal financial assistance application and reporting requirements, and streamline the coordination among agencies responsible for delivering public services. Much of the act's provisions have been implemented, including the creation of an electronic application system for federal grants. That system began with the launch of Grants.gov, the federal government's portal for grantseekers and grant managers.

Private Sector Trends

Let's not forget about private sector philanthropy. Foundations have been making grants for decades. In declining economic times, foundations worked aggressively to fund various programs when federal funding decreased or federal priorities shifted.

According to the Foundation Center, the growth of new foundations over the decades has been at a record-breaking pace – especially in the late 1980s and early 1990s. Many private sector grantmakers (foundations and corporations) report that they've seen an increase in charitable giving in recent years and attribute at least some of that growth to individual wealth transfer. For example, between 1991 and 1994, new gifts to foundations grew 36 percent, to a record $8.1 billion in 1994. For the top 100 foundations in the United States, this trend has continued into this decade. Moreover, private philanthropic

©Thompson Publishing Group

organizations with large endowments, such as the Bill and Melinda Gates Foundation, are increasingly awarding funding through other transfer of wealth streams.

And these private and corporate foundations are increasingly streamlining their grant application mechanisms by launching their own e-grants systems for researching and applying for grants.

Organizations can prepare themselves for today's grantseeking trends by subscribing to grant funding opportunity alerts that reduce or eliminate time-consuming funding research, and realizing that all types of grantmakers are working aggressively to reduce paperwork by converting the grant application process from hard copy to electronic grant application submissions.

About This Book

The purpose of *Winning Strategies for Developing Grant Proposals* is to help organizations that search for funding – state and local governments, community organizations, school districts, universities, hospitals, and other nonprofit organizations – fine-tune their grantseeking skills and practices and get the latest intelligence on what it takes to win a grant award in today's highly competitive funding environment. Here's an overview of what readers can expect to take away from each information-filled chapter.

Chapter 2 - Beginning the Grantseeking Process. After reading this chapter, you'll have the skills needed to understand your organization's responsibilities when you apply for and accept grants. You'll also hone critical thinking skills when it comes to analyzing the cost of administering grant awards. You'll have a better understanding of the many strings attached to different kinds of grant awards. You'll build skills in readying your organization for the steps it needs to take before even starting to look for a grant. You'll develop keen research skills needed to identify the various resources available to help you pinpoint the most appropriate funding sources for your organization's projects. You'll also get guidance on deciding whether to hire a grants professional to assist you in planning, researching and writing grant proposals. Finally, you'll finish Chapter 2 with in-depth knowledge on how to set up a grant proposal "library" and how to use the Freedom of Information Act to enhance your grantseeking skills.

Chapter 3 - Navigating the Online Federal Grants Process. This chapter gives you all of the e-grant skills you'll need to maneuver Grants.gov with professional confidence. You'll build skills in how to obtain a DUNS number for your organization. You'll also quickly gain and store valuable knowledge about why the government requires that all e-grant applicants register their organization's with the Central Contractor Registry (CCR). After reading about what type of information you'll need to gather, you'll be ready to start the CCR process for your organization. In just a short time you'll be able to authorize a representative to serve as a liaison with Grants.gov. You'll learn the ins and outs of setting up daily Grants.gov e-mail alerts highlighting the newest funding opportunities and how to search for federal grant opportunities four different ways. And, just when you thought you had learned everything about Grants.gov, you'll become an expert in how to use PureView – a free program Grants.gov uses to provide access to the grant application – from installation on your computer system to completing applications offline to uploading your information online to tracking your application after it's been submitted.

Chapter 4 – Basics of Good Proposal Writing. In this chapter, you'll discover dozens of tips and skill building approaches to writing solid, sound and successful grant proposals. You'll learn about the importance of each section of a grant proposal and develop a better understanding of what grantmakers look for in each section of your application packages. You'll discover how much research and other advance work is required before you even start to write your proposals. Your skills will soar when you read the "A to Z" successful grant proposal writing tips. Finally, this chapter will provide you with new skills for writing a persuasive proposal narrative.

Chapter 5 – Winning Grants from Private Sector Sources. This chapter focuses on the numerous private sector sources that are available to fund a variety of programs. The chapter begins with a brief history of 21st century giving patterns. You'll quickly build your knowledge about the various types of private sector funding sources – private foundations, community foundations, corporate giving programs, etc. In the section on how corporations and foundations fund government programs, from the federal level all the way down to local governments, you'll improve your understanding of these grantmakers' objectives. By the end of this chapter, you'll know how to research private sector grantmakers so your proposals for one-time or ongoing project support actually market themselves to the funder's philanthropic values. I've included some real-life examples of how to successfully approach private sector funders for grant funding as well as specific grant proposals that were selected for funding support.

Chapter 6 – Winning Grants from Federal Agencies. This chapter serves as the primer for anyone searching for funding from the federal government. You'll discover how the federal budget and appropriation processes work and the types of funding available from the federal government. You'll increase your understanding of how grant applications are solicited and the Web sites that will keep you up to date on federal grant funding opportunities. You'll get one more overview of Grants.gov, from its early beginnings to its systemic capacity today. You'll learn what federal grant officers look for in winning grant applications. By the end of the chapter, you'll have an increased understanding of how to write federal grant applications from an insider's perspective and learn about the benefits of participating in the federal peer review process.

Chapter 7 – Why Some Proposals Fail. In reading this chapter, you'll have an eye opening experience about why grantmakers reject more proposals than they fund. You'll discover the fatal errors to avoid and how to find out from public and private sector grantmakers why your proposal wasn't funded. You'll gain new insight about how the human element affects grantseeking. Finally, you'll read some advice from grant award winners on how to convince field readers, peer review panels and grant officials that your organization is prepared to take on and successfully manage a grant funded project.

©Thompson Publishing Group

Chapter 8 – Forms to Use When Seeking Grant Funds. This chapter includes the standard grant application forms needed to apply for federal funding. You'll also take a visual tour of a commonly used foundation grant application. Also provided in this chapter is a list of regional associations with state- or region-specific grant writing forms and formats.

Chapter 9 – Resources for Grantseekers. This last chapter gives you top notch guidance on the resources available to grantseekers. You'll find sources of information on private sector grants and Web site addresses for the top 100 foundations in the United States. You'll also find a list of the Foundation Center's Cooperating Libraries, which are located in hundreds of communities nationwide. To close out this chapter and the final step in helping you to build your grantseeking skills, I've included some online resources to federal grant writing and funding opportunity announcements.

Beginning the Grantseeking Process

2

For many organizations, getting a grant award can seem like the solution to all of their financial problems. For other organizations, government grants are viewed as laden with red tape and too many strings. These organizations do not want to give up their freedom when it comes to spending monies or moving a dollar from one line item to the next without the grantor's written permission. Executive directors have heard horror stories from their nonprofit colleagues and they've simply decided to exist off of private sector grant awards and individual contributions. What are they failing to realize? Every funder – public or private sector – expects and requires high levels of accountability. After all, funders are accountable to someone too!

Where do you start to begin the grantseeking process? Well, you certainly don't start by first, finding a grant funding opportunity, and second, immediately writing the application. There are a lot of steps to take in between finding the money and applying for the money.

Accountability Issues to Consider

Applying for a federal grant is a massive undertaking for any organization that hasn't previously familiarized itself with all of the regulatory requirements. First, your organization must start the federal grantseeking process with an understanding of the approach needed to obtain public dollars with strings attached.

1. Your organization must be willing to use the grant funds only for the intended purposes of the grant program.

2. Your organization must will willing to accept its role as a diligent steward of federal funds by making sure that the projects funded remain in good standing with the awarding agency.

3. Your organization must be willing to designate staff who can review the grant application's guidance documents as well as the program-specific regulations and requirements. In turn, the staff must be able to highlight concerns and review them with all levels of administration, from the finance director to the program directors to the organization's attorney.

Next, we'll look at the guidance documents and regulations that apply to your grant project.

Program Regulations. Program regulations typically will be identified in the Federal Register or Grants.gov notice announcing the grant competition or in the larger grant application package. Each program has a set of regulations that govern how projects are to be implemented by grantees. Some programs may have very detailed guidance concerning allowable and unallowable costs, spending caps on specific budget categories and staffing requirements. For example, a program might require a project director to work fulltime on the project. But other programs may have only a few program-specific regulations.

Here's an example of program regulations (also labeled as program requirements by some federal grantmaking agencies) from grant applications guidelines published by the U.S. Department of Health and Human Services for its Maternal and Child Health (MCH) Bureau – Health Resources and Services Administration (HRSA):

Program requirements of this cooperative agreement include:

*   monitor and evaluate project activities to determine if services are being delivered in a timely manner with an emphasis on quality service delivery;

*   timely completion of activities approved by HRSA that were proposed in response to application review criteria listed in this application guidance;

*   provide technical assistance and training opportunities; and produce and disseminate materials including publishing articles as appropriate;

*   update training materials quarterly based on new findings;

*   participation in face-to-face meetings and conference calls with the federal office conducted during the period of the cooperative agreement;

*   collaborate with the federal office in an ongoing review of activities, procedures and budget items, information/publication prior to dissemination and contracts;

*   expand "Risky Drinking" model to additional Community Health Cares (CHCs) systems;

*   provide technical assistance on Fetal Alcohol Spectrum Disorders (FASD) to CHCs and MCH sites;

*   collaborate with Title V and MCH sites in selected states;

©Thompson Publishing Group

- adapt training materials for MCH sites;

- facilitate coordination of activities between CHCs and MCH sites; and

- create a system of prevention, identification and support of individuals with FASD in CHCs and MCH sites.

You'll note that this announcement is for a cooperative agreement; it's the same as a grant award. Also, there are a lot of acronyms in this announcement. This means you'll need to familiarize yourself with the grantmaking agency's tech talk in order to understand the magnitude of your organization's responsibilities.

Standard Assurances. Every federal grant applicant is asked to demonstrate their intent to comply with standard assurances. This means your organization must be willing to assure and certify that it will comply with all federal statutes, regulations, policies, guidelines and requirements, including the Office of Management and Budget (OMB) circulars. The assurances are full of legal clauses and if you don't sign off, it could result in your organization not passing the initial technical review of the grant application (a check for inclusion of signed forms and adherence to the application's writing and packaging format).

An example of a standard assurance follows on pages 10-11.

FIG. 2-1

OMB Approval No. 0348-0040

ASSURANCES - NON-CONSTRUCTION PROGRAMS

Public reporting burden for this collection of information is estimated to average 15 minutes per response, including time for reviewing instructions, searching existing data sources, gathering and maintaining the data needed, and completing and reviewing the collection of information. Send comments regarding the burden estimate or any other aspect of this collection of information, including suggestions for reducing this burden, to the Office of Management and Budget, Paperwork Reduction Project (0348-0040), Washington, DC 20503.

PLEASE DO NOT RETURN YOUR COMPLETED FORM TO THE OFFICE OF MANAGEMENT AND BUDGET. SEND IT TO THE ADDRESS PROVIDED BY THE SPONSORING AGENCY.

NOTE: Certain of these assurances may not be applicable to your project or program. If you have questions, please contact the awarding agency. Further, certain Federal awarding agencies may require applicants to certify to additional assurances. If such is the case, you will be notified.

As the duly authorized representative of the applicant, I certify that the applicant:

1. Has the legal authority to apply for Federal assistance and the institutional, managerial and financial capability (including funds sufficient to pay the non-Federal share of project cost) to ensure proper planning, management and completion of the project described in this application.

2. Will give the awarding agency, the Comptroller General of the United States and, if appropriate, the State, through any authorized representative, access to and the right to examine all records, books, papers, or documents related to the award; and will establish a proper accounting system in accordance with generally accepted accounting standards or agency directives.

3. Will establish safeguards to prohibit employees from using their positions for a purpose that constitutes or presents the appearance of personal or organizational conflict of interest, or personal gain.

4. Will initiate and complete the work within the applicable time frame after receipt of approval of the awarding agency.

5. Will comply with the Intergovernmental Personnel Act of 1970 (42 U.S.C. §§4728-4763) relating to prescribed standards for merit systems for programs funded under one of the 19 statutes or regulations specified in Appendix A of OPM's Standards for a Merit System of Personnel Administration (5 C.F.R. 900, Subpart F).

6. Will comply with all Federal statutes relating to nondiscrimination. These include but are not limited to: (a) Title VI of the Civil Rights Act of 1964 (P.L. 88-352) which prohibits discrimination on the basis of race, color or national origin; (b) Title IX of the Education Amendments of 1972, as amended (20 U.S.C. §§1681-1683, and 1685-1686), which prohibits discrimination on the basis of sex; (c) Section 504 of the Rehabilitation Act of 1973, as amended (29 U.S.C. §794), which prohibits discrimination on the basis of handicaps; (d) the Age Discrimination Act of 1975, as amended (42 U.S.C. §§6101-6107), which prohibits discrimination on the basis of age; (e) the Drug Abuse Office and Treatment Act of 1972 (P.L. 92-255), as amended, relating to nondiscrimination on the basis of drug abuse; (f) the Comprehensive Alcohol Abuse and Alcoholism Prevention, Treatment and Rehabilitation Act of 1970 (P.L. 91-616), as amended, relating to nondiscrimination on the basis of alcohol abuse or alcoholism; (g) §§523 and 527 of the Public Health Service Act of 1912 (42 U.S.C. §§290 dd-3 and 290 ee 3), as amended, relating to confidentiality of alcohol and drug abuse patient records; (h) Title VIII of the Civil Rights Act of 1968 (42 U.S.C. §§3601 et seq.), as amended, relating to nondiscrimination in the sale, rental or financing of housing; (i) any other nondiscrimination provisions in the specific statute(s) under which application for Federal assistance is being made; and, (j) the requirements of any other nondiscrimination statute(s) which may apply to the application.

7. Will comply, or has already complied, with the requirements of Titles II and III of the Uniform Relocation Assistance and Real Property Acquisition Policies Act of 1970 (P.L. 91-646) which provide for fair and equitable treatment of persons displaced or whose property is acquired as a result of Federal or federally-assisted programs. These requirements apply to all interests in real property acquired for project purposes regardless of Federal participation in purchases.

8. Will comply, as applicable, with provisions of the Hatch Act (5 U.S.C. §§1501-1508 and 7324-7328) which limit the political activities of employees whose principal employment activities are funded in whole or in part with Federal funds.

Previous Edition Usable

Authorized for Local Reproduction

Standard Form 424B (Rev. 7-97)
Prescribed by OMB Circular A-102

©Thompson Publishing Group

FIG. 2-1 (continued)

9. Will comply, as applicable, with the provisions of the Davis-Bacon Act (40 U.S.C. §§276a to 276a-7), the Copeland Act (40 U.S.C. §276c and 18 U.S.C. §874), and the Contract Work Hours and Safety Standards Act (40 U.S.C. §§327-333), regarding labor standards for federally-assisted construction subagreements.

10. Will comply, if applicable, with flood insurance purchase requirements of Section 102(a) of the Flood Disaster Protection Act of 1973 (P.L. 93-234) which requires recipients in a special flood hazard area to participate in the program and to purchase flood insurance if the total cost of insurable construction and acquisition is $10,000 or more.

11. Will comply with environmental standards which may be prescribed pursuant to the following: (a) institution of environmental quality control measures under the National Environmental Policy Act of 1969 (P.L. 91-190) and Executive Order (EO) 11514; (b) notification of violating facilities pursuant to EO 11738; (c) protection of wetlands pursuant to EO 11990; (d) evaluation of flood hazards in floodplains in accordance with EO 11988; (e) assurance of project consistency with the approved State management program developed under the Coastal Zone Management Act of 1972 (16 U.S.C. §§1451 et seq.); (f) conformity of Federal actions to State (Clean Air) Implementation Plans under Section 176(c) of the Clean Air Act of 1955, as amended (42 U.S.C. §§7401 et seq.); (g) protection of underground sources of drinking water under the Safe Drinking Water Act of 1974, as amended (P.L. 93-523); and, (h) protection of endangered species under the Endangered Species Act of 1973, as amended (P.L. 93-205).

12. Will comply with the Wild and Scenic Rivers Act of 1968 (16 U.S.C. §§1271 et seq.) related to protecting components or potential components of the national wild and scenic rivers system.

13. Will assist the awarding agency in assuring compliance with Section 106 of the National Historic Preservation Act of 1966, as amended (16 U.S.C. §470), EO 11593 (identification and protection of historic properties), and the Archaeological and Historic Preservation Act of 1974 (16 U.S.C. §§469a-1 et seq.).

14. Will comply with P.L. 93-348 regarding the protection of human subjects involved in research, development, and related activities supported by this award of assistance.

15. Will comply with the Laboratory Animal Welfare Act of 1966 (P.L. 89-544, as amended, 7 U.S.C. §§2131 et seq.) pertaining to the care, handling, and treatment of warm blooded animals held for research, teaching, or other activities supported by this award of assistance.

16. Will comply with the Lead-Based Paint Poisoning Prevention Act (42 U.S.C. §§4801 et seq.) which prohibits the use of lead-based paint in construction or rehabilitation of residence structures.

17. Will cause to be performed the required financial and compliance audits in accordance with the Single Audit Act Amendments of 1996 and OMB Circular No. A-133, "Audits of States, Local Governments, and Non-Profit Organizations."

18. Will comply with all applicable requirements of all other Federal laws, executive orders, regulations, and policies governing this program.

SIGNATURE OF AUTHORIZED CERTIFYING OFFICIAL	TITLE
APPLICANT ORGANIZATION	DATE SUBMITTED

Standard Form 424B (Rev. 7-97) Back

Certification Regarding Debarment and Suspension

Your organization must certify that it is not presently debarred, suspended, ineligible or voluntarily excluded from covered lower tier transactions ($25,000 for any single transaction) by a state or federal court. If an organization had previously received a state or federal grant award and committed fraud or theft that resulted in court-involved legal actions initiated by the grantmaking agency, then you would not be able to sign off on this certification form. By signing, your organization is certifying that its grant management practices meet federal standards for managing public funds.

Fig. 2-2 is an example of how this form looks (it's included in all federal grant applications and usually downloadable from the grantmaking agency's Web site).

©Thompson Publishing Group

FIG. 2-2

Certification Regarding Debarment, Suspension, Ineligibility and Voluntary Exclusion — Lower Tier Covered Transactions

This certification is required by the Department of Education regulations implementing Executive Order 12549, Debarment and Suspension, 34 CFR Part 85, for all lower tier transactions meeting the threshold and tier requirements stated at Section 85.110.

Instructions for Certification

1. By signing and submitting this proposal, the prospective lower tier participant is providing the certification set out below.

2. The certification in this clause is a material representation of fact upon which reliance was placed when this transaction was entered into. If it is later determined that the prospective lower tier participant knowingly rendered an erroneous certification, in addition to other remedies available to the Federal Government, the department or agency with which this transaction originated may pursue available remedies, including suspension and/or debarment.

3. The prospective lower tier participant shall provide immediate written notice to the person to which this proposal is submitted if at any time the prospective lower tier participant learns that its certification was erroneous when submitted or has become erroneous by reason of changed circumstances.

4. The terms "covered transaction," "debarred," "suspended," "ineligible," "lower tier covered transaction," "participant," " person," "primary covered transaction," " principal," "proposal," and "voluntarily excluded," as used in this clause, have the meanings set out in the Definitions and Coverage sections of rules implementing Executive Order 12549. You may contact the person to which this proposal is submitted for assistance in obtaining a copy of those regulations.

5. The prospective lower tier participant agrees by submitting this proposal that, should the proposed covered transaction be entered into, it shall not knowingly enter into any lower tier covered transaction with a person who is debarred, suspended, declared ineligible, or voluntarily excluded from participation in this covered transaction, unless authorized by the department or agency with which this transaction originated.

6. The prospective lower tier participant further agrees by submitting this proposal that it will include the clause titled "Certification Regarding Debarment, Suspension, Ineligibility, and Voluntary Exclusion-Lower Tier Covered Transactions," without modification, in all lower tier covered transactions and in all solicitations for lower tier covered transactions.

7. A participant in a covered transaction may rely upon a certification of a prospective participant in a lower tier covered transaction that it is not debarred, suspended, ineligible, or voluntarily excluded from the covered transaction, unless it knows that the certification is erroneous. A participant may decide the method and frequency by which it determines the eligibility of its principals. Each participant may but is not required to, check the Nonprocurement List.

8. Nothing contained in the foregoing shall be construed to require establishment of a system of records in order to render in good faith the certification required by this clause. The knowledge and information of a participant is not required to exceed that which is normally possessed by a prudent person in the ordinary course of business dealings.

9. Except for transactions authorized under paragraph 5 of these instructions, if a participant in a covered transaction knowingly enters into a lower tier covered transaction with a person who is suspended, debarred, ineligible, or voluntarily excluded from participation in this transaction, in addition to other remedies available to the Federal Government, the department or agency with which this transaction originated may pursue available remedies, including suspension and/or debarment.

Certification

(1) The prospective lower tier participant certifies, by submission of this proposal, that neither it nor its principals are presently debarred, suspended, proposed for debarment, declared ineligible, or voluntarily excluded from participation in this transaction by any Federal department or agency.

(2) Where the prospective lower tier participant is unable to certify to any of the statements in this certification, such prospective participant shall attach an explanation to this proposal.

NAME OF APPLICANT	PR/AWARD NUMBER AND/OR PROJECT NAME
PRINTED NAME AND TITLE OF AUTHORIZED REPRESENTATIVE	
SIGNATURE	DATE

ED 80-0014, 9/90 (Replaces GCS-009 (REV.12/88), which is obsolete)

Lobbying Certification. First and foremost, you cannot use federal grant monies to hire a lobbying firm to sway your state or federal elected officials to draft legislation that will result in favors or financial gifts for your organization. Lobbying is not illegal; you just can't pay for it with federal funds. Lobbying funds can, however, come from the private sector. Many large nonprofit organizations have lobbying firms on contract. By signing off on the lobbying certification form, your organization is promising the government that no federal funds have been paid or will be paid, by or on behalf of your organization, to any person for influencing or attempting to influence an officer or employee of any government agency, a member of Congress, or an employee of a member of Congress in connection with the making of any federal grant. In other words, you cannot use a lobbyist to sway the grantmaking agency's decision toward funding your grant award.

There are two lobbying certification forms. The first (Fig. 2-3) reveals current lobbying activities if your organization is represented by a lobbying firm at the time the grant application is submitted. The second (Fig. 2-4) is a certification stating that your organization will not use any federal funds to hire a lobbyist. These forms can be downloaded from the grantmaking agency's Web site or from OMB's Web site.

FIG. 2-3

DISCLOSURE OF LOBBYING ACTIVITIES

Complete this form to disclose lobbying activities pursuant to 31 U.S.C. 1352

(See reverse for public burden disclosure.)

Approved by OMB
0348-0046

1. Type of Federal Action: a. contract b. grant c. cooperative agreement d. loan e. loan guarantee f. loan insurance	2. Status of Federal Action: a. bid/offer/application b. initial award c. post-award	3. Report Type: a. initial filing b. material change **For Material Change Only:** year _____ quarter _____ date of last report _____
4. Name and Address of Reporting Entity: ☐ Prime ☐ Subawardee Tier _____, *if known*: Congressional District, *if known*:	5. If Reporting Entity in No. 4 is a Subawardee, Enter Name and Address of Prime: Congressional District, *if known*:	
6. Federal Department/Agency:	7. Federal Program Name/Description: CFDA Number, *if applicable*: _____	
8. Federal Action Number, *if known*:	9. Award Amount, *if known*: $	
10. a. Name and Address of Lobbying Registrant (*if individual, last name, first name, MI*):	b. Individuals Performing Services (*including address if different from No. 10a*) (*last name, first name, MI*):	
11. Information requested through this form is authorized by title 31 U.S.C. section 1352. This disclosure of lobbying activities is a material representation of fact upon which reliance was placed by the tier above when this transaction was made or entered into. This disclosure is required pursuant to 31 U.S.C. 1352. This information will be reported to the Congress semi-annually and will be available for public inspection. Any person who fails to file the required disclosure shall be subject to a civil penalty of not less that $10,000 and not more than $100,000 for each such failure.	Signature: _____ Print Name: _____ Title: _____ Telephone No.: _____ Date: _____	
Federal Use Only:	Authorized for Local Reproduction Standard Form LLL (Rev. 7-97)	

©Thompson Publishing Group

FIG. 2-3 (continued)

INSTRUCTIONS FOR COMPLETION OF SF-LLL, DISCLOSURE OF LOBBYING ACTIVITIES

This disclosure form shall be completed by the reporting entity, whether subawardee or prime Federal recipient, at the initiation or receipt of a covered Federal action, or a material change to a previous filing, pursuant to title 31 U.S.C. section 1352. The filing of a form is required for each payment or agreement to make payment to any lobbying entity for influencing or attempting to influence an officer or employee of any agency, a Member of Congress, an officer or employee of Congress, or an employee of a Member of Congress in connection with a covered Federal action. Complete all items that apply for both the initial filing and material change report. Refer to the implementing guidance published by the Office of Management and Budget for additional information.

1. Identify the type of covered Federal action for which lobbying activity is and/or has been secured to influence the outcome of a covered Federal action.

2. Identify the status of the covered Federal action.

3. Identify the appropriate classification of this report. If this is a followup report caused by a material change to the information previously reported, enter the year and quarter in which the change occurred. Enter the date of the last previously submitted report by this reporting entity for this covered Federal action.

4. Enter the full name, address, city, State and zip code of the reporting entity. Include Congressional District, if known. Check the appropriate classification of the reporting entity that designates if it is, or expects to be, a prime or subaward recipient. Identify the tier of the subawardee, e.g., the first subawardee of the prime is the 1st tier. Subawards include but are not limited to subcontracts, subgrants and contract awards under grants.

5. If the organization filing the report in item 4 checks "Subawardee," then enter the full name, address, city, State and zip code of the prime Federal recipient. Include Congressional District, if known.

6. Enter the name of the Federal agency making the award or loan commitment. Include at least one organizational level below agency name, if known. For example, Department of Transportation, United States Coast Guard.

7. Enter the Federal program name or description for the covered Federal action (item 1). If known, enter the full Catalog of Federal Domestic Assistance (CFDA) number for grants, cooperative agreements, loans, and loan commitments.

8. Enter the most appropriate Federal identifying number available for the Federal action identified in item 1 (e.g., Request for Proposal (RFP) number; Invitation for Bid (IFB) number; grant announcement number; the contract, grant, or loan award number; the application/proposal control number assigned by the Federal agency). Include prefixes, e.g., "RFP-DE-90-001."

9. For a covered Federal action where there has been an award or loan commitment by the Federal agency, enter the Federal amount of the award/loan commitment for the prime entity identified in item 4 or 5.

10. (a) Enter the full name, address, city, State and zip code of the lobbying registrant under the Lobbying Disclosure Act of 1995 engaged by the reporting entity identified in item 4 to influence the covered Federal action.

    (b) Enter the full names of the individual(s) performing services, and include full address if different from 10 (a). Enter Last Name, First Name, and Middle Initial (MI).

11. The certifying official shall sign and date the form, print his/her name, title, and telephone number.

According to the Paperwork Reduction Act, as amended, no persons are required to respond to a collection of information unless it displays a valid OMB Control Number. The valid OMB control number for this information collection is OMB No. 0348-0046. Public reporting burden for this collection of information is estimated to average 10 minutes per response, including time for reviewing instructions, searching existing data sources, gathering and maintaining the data needed, and completing and reviewing the collection of information. Send comments regarding the burden estimate or any other aspect of this collection of information, including suggestions for reducing this burden, to the Office of Management and Budget, Paperwork Reduction Project (0348-0046), Washington, DC 20503.

FIG. 2-4

CERTIFICATION REGARDING LOBBYING

Applicants must review the requirements for certification regarding lobbying included in the regulations cited below before completing this form. Applicants must sign this form to comply with the certification requirements under 34 CFR Part 82, "New Restrictions on Lobbying." This certification is a material representation of fact upon which the Department of Education relies when it makes a grant or enters into a cooperative agreement.

As required by Section 1352, Title 31 of the U.S. Code, and implemented at 34 CFR Part 82, for persons entering into a Federal contract, grant or cooperative agreement over $100,000, as defined at 34 CFR Part 82, Sections 82.105 and 82.110, the applicant certifies that:

(a) No Federal appropriated funds have been paid or will be paid, by or on behalf of the undersigned, to any person for influencing or attempting to influence an officer or employee of any agency, a Member of Congress, an officer or employee of Congress, or an employee of a Member of Congress in connection with the making of any Federal grant, the entering into of any cooperative agreement, and the extension, continuation, renewal, amendment, or modification of any Federal grant or cooperative agreement;

(b) If any funds other than Federal appropriated funds have been paid or will be paid to any person for influencing or attempting to influence an officer or employee of any agency, a Member of Congress, an officer or employee of Congress, or an employee of a Member of Congress in connection with this Federal grant or cooperative agreement, the undersigned shall complete and submit Standard Form - LLL, "Disclosure Form to Report Lobbying," in accordance with its instructions;

(c) The undersigned shall require that the language of this certification be included in the award documents for all subawards at all tiers (including subgrants and contracts under grants and cooperative agreements) and that all subrecipients shall certify and disclose accordingly.

As the duly authorized representative of the applicant, I hereby certify that the applicant will comply with the above certification.

NAME OF APPLICANT	PR/AWARD NUMBER AND / OR PROJECT NAME
PRINTED NAME AND TITLE OF AUTHORIZED REPRESENTATIVE	
SIGNATURE	DATE

ED 80-0013

06/04

©Thompson Publishing Group

Drug-Free Workplace Certification. This certification must also be signed by your organization's representative. The certification holds or binds your organization to maintain a workplace where none of the employees use drugs for illegal purposes on the premises. I bet you've been driving down the road in your community and seen signs on a post near the roadside that read, Drug Free Community. This means that the community is working toward no illegal drug use within its municipal boundaries. By signing off on this certification, your organization is certifying that it maintains a drug-free workplace, notifies its employees of the policies, has established a drug-free awareness program, and makes it a requirement that each employee working under the grant-funded program receive a statement of the conditions for a drug-free workplace. Fig. 2-5 is an example of this certification.

FIG. 2-5

OMB APPROVAL NO.
9000 - 0101

U.S. DEPARTMENT OF AGRICULTURE

**CERTIFICATION REGARDING
DRUG-FREE WORKPLACE REQUIREMENTS (GRANTS)
ALTERNATIVE I - FOR GRANTEES OTHER THAN INDIVIDUALS**

This certification is required by the regulations implementing Sections 5151-5160 of the Drug-Free Workplace Act of 1988 (Pub. L. 100-690, Title V, Subtitle D; 41 U.S.C. 701 et seq.), 7 CFR Part 3017, Subpart F, Section 3017.600, Purpose. The regulations were published as Part II of the January 31,1989 Federal Register (pages 4947-4952). Copies of the regulations may be obtained by contacting the Department of Agriculture agency offering the grant.

(BEFORE COMPLETING CERTIFICATION, READ INSTRUCTIONS ON REVERSE)

Alternative I

(A) The grantee certifies that it will provide a drug-free workplace by:

    (a) Publishing a statement notifying employees that the unlawful manufacture, distribution, dispensing, possession or use of a controlled substance is prohibited in the grantee's workplace and specifying the actions that will be taken against employees for violation of such prohibition;

    (b) Establishing a drug-free awareness program to inform employees about --

        (1) The dangers of drug abuse in the workplace;

        (2) The grantee's policy of maintaining a drug-free workplace;

        (3) Any available drug counseling, rehabilitation, and employee assistance programs; and

        (4) The penalties that may be imposed upon employees for drug abuse violations occurring in the workplace;

    (c) Making it a requirement that each employee to be engaged in the performance of the grant be given a copy of the statement required by paragraph (a);

    (d) Notifying the employee in the statement required by paragraph (a) that, as a condition of employment under the grant, the employee will --

        (1) Abide by the terms of the statement; and

FIG. 2-5 (continued)

(2) Notify the employer of any criminal drug statute conviction for a violation occurring in the workplace no later than five days after such conviction;

(e) Notifying the agency within ten days after receiving notice under subparagraph (d)(2) from an employee or otherwise receiving actual notice of such conviction;

(f) Taking one of the following actions, within 30 days of receiving notice under subparagraph (d)(2), with respect to any employee who is so convicted --

   (1) Taking appropriate personnel action against such an employee, up to and including termination; or

   (2) Requiring such employee to participate satisfactorily in a drug abuse assistance or rehabilitation program approved for such purposes by a Federal, State, or local health, law enforcement, or other appropriate agency;

(g) Making a good faith effort to continue to maintain a drug-free workplace through implementation of paragraphs (a), (b), (c), (d), (e) and (f).

B. The grantee shall insert in the space provided below the site(s) for the performance of work done in connection with the specific grant.

Place of Performance (Street address, city, county, State, zip code)

_____

_____

_____

_____
Organization Name   PR/Award Number or Project Name

_____
Name and Title of Authorized Representative

_____
Signature   Date

INSTRUCTIONS FOR CERTIFICATION

1. By signing and submitting this form, the grantee is providing the certification set out on pages 1 and 2.

2. The certification set out on pages 1 and 2 is a material representation of fact upon which reliance was placed when the agency determined to award the grant. If it is later determined that the grantee knowingly rendered a false certification, or otherwise violates the requirements of the Drug-Free Workplace Act, the agency, in addition to any other remedies available to the Federal Government, may take action authorized under the Drug-Free Workplace Act.

2

©Thompson Publishing Group

You're not through learning about grant applicant accountability yet. Next, I'll cover some of the legal obligations that come with applying for and receiving federal grant monies.

Legal Issues to Consider

Financial Reporting Requirements. To make sure that grant funds are used properly, organizations that receive federal funds must file regular financial status reports. These forms do not take long to fill out, but they are important. The basic financial report form is a one-page document called Standard Form 269. Many federal grantmaking agencies have adapted this form to suit their own programs. You can find a copy of Standard Form 269 at www.white-house.gov/omb/grants/grants_ forms.html.

> Remember to include a line item in your grant application budget for the cost to prepare financial reports.

Cost-sharing/Matching. These are two terms that often are used interchangeably. Certain programs have a requirement that grant applicants pledge that they will contribute a certain level of financial support to the project once they are awarded grants and become grantees. The amount of financial support varies from program to program, and not all grant programs have cost-sharing or matching requirements. Whether cost-sharing or matching requirements apply to a particular program will be noted in the Federal Register or Grants.gov notice that announces a grant competition for that program.

Depending on the particular program, a grantee's cost-share or match may be made in cash, in an in-kind contribution (such as facilities, equipment and supplies), or in staff time. For example, a program may require a 50 percent match from its grantees. That means that, if a grantee receives a $100,000 award, it will have to bring to the project an additional $50,000 in either cash or some type of in-kind contribution.

> Private sector funders (corporations and foundations) often invite proposals for cost-share or matching funds. Identify potential private sector funding sources, call, and inquire about grant opportunities.

Before your organization moves forward on a grant application that requires cost-sharing/matching, be sure to work with your financial staff to determine where the cost-share or match will come from. It <u>cannot</u> be taken from another federal grant award that your organization has received and is still administering.

Recordkeeping. Your organization will be required to maintain financial and programmatic records for your project for up to three years following the project's conclusion. For example, if you received a grant for a three-year project period that began on Oct. 1, 2003, and ended on Sept, 30, 2006, you would be required to maintain all of the records regarding that grant until Sept. 30, 2009.

> Both government grantmaking agencies and private sector funders expect your organization to maintain financial records for an acceptable period of time.

Performance Reporting. Typically, all federal grantees will be required to submit to the awarding agency both periodic (usually annually) and final performance reports that detail the project's accomplishments, as well as any shortcomings. The awarding agency provides instructions as to the format and the degree of detail that needs to be included in these reports. For grant projects funded for only one year, only a single report may be required. Along with performance reports, some programs require grantees to participate in national evaluation surveys. Such surveys provide information on the national need for and the impact of this particular grant program.

> Before you make the decision to apply for federal grant funds, make sure your organization is ready to commit to post-grant award evaluations such as required audits and other reviews.

Audit. All organizations that receive federal funds are subject to basic audit requirements. The audits are necessary to make sure that federal dollars have been spent properly on legitimate costs. It is therefore extremely important for your organization to keep accurate records of all transactions conducted with federal funds.

Most organizations are not audited by the government itself, although the federal government has the right to audit any program that receives public money at any time. For organizations that spend a total of $500,000 or more in federal funds (calculated based on awards from all federal programs) – an audit by a private, independent outside legal or accounting firm is required. More information on audits may be found on OMB's Web site (www.whitehouse.gov/omb/circulars). OMB Circular A-133 explains the Single Audit Act requirements for federal grantees.

Purchasing Equipment With Federal Grant Funds. In many cases, organizations receiving a federal grant award are allowed to keep the items they purchase after the grant is over so that they may continue running the project without federal funds and because it simply would not be cost effective for the government to remove the items from one grantee and give them to others. There are instances, however, when the government will take title to items, such as research equipment, from a former grantee and provide the items to a new grantee that will be completing the grant project.

Sanctions for Violating Federal Rules. If your organization violates the requirements specified in your grant agreement or otherwise improperly uses the federal funds it receives, the organization may be subject to legal action. Among other things, it could lose the grant funds, be required to repay the funds received and pay any damages that might be awarded through court action. If your organization uses its funds fraudulently, it could be subject to criminal prosecution.

> Before your organization decides to proceed with writing and submitting a federal grant application, make sure to check the specific terms and conditions of the grant funding program. If you have any questions, check with the federal program contact person.

©Thompson Publishing Group

Program Evaluation

Federal and private sector grantmakers require some form of program evaluation. The requirements for evaluation are clearly spelled out in the grant application guidelines. Evaluations may be conducted by one of your internal staff members, an evaluation consultant or firm, or both. Before your organization decides to apply for a grant, make sure you understand the grantmaker's full expectations for the evaluation process. Some federal agencies require that your organization participate in a national program evaluation and that your key program staff attend technical assistance training meetings. The evaluation process required is detailed and is usually qualitative and quantitative. Both public and private sector funders allow you to include the cost of evaluation in your project budget.

> Before you proceed with any federal grant competition, consider the financial and human resources needed to meet requirements.

Grant Management Costs to Consider

Federal grant awards often come with strings attached and your organization must be ready to meet the many administrative and program requirements imposed by the grantmaking agency. It will cost your organization money to manage a federal grant award. Some of the costs to consider include:

- **Financial recordkeeping.** Many grantee organizations assign to an in-house staff person fiscal accounting and recordkeeping for grant awards. Often, organizations will retain a public accounting firm to help them manage their federal funds in accordance with their grant agreement and federal financial management requirements. Remember, you'll need to build money into your project budget to cover these costs.

- **Financial reporting.** It will cost money to have a staff person prepare all of the financial reports required by federal grantmaking agencies. Think about who will be assigned this task and how much time this person will devote to this grant management requirement. You'll need to build money into your project budget to cover these costs.

- **Mandatory meetings with funding agencies.** Many federal grantmaking agencies require at least one meeting each year at the funder's headquarters. Often these meetings cover how to fill out electronic reporting forms, problems with previous reports, how to set up the electronic funds transfer process, and more. You'll need to build monies into your project budget to cover staff travel expenses for these mandatory meetings.

- **Cost reimbursement grant agreements.** Most federal grantmaking agencies will advance the first quarter's project expenses to your organization as soon as you have signed a grant agreement. However, some federal grantmaking agencies operate on a cost reimbursement basis. This means your organization must have the monies upfront to cover each quarter's project expenses. Once your financial staff has submitted proof of project expenditures, the grantmaking agency transfers the allowable costs into your organization's bank account.

- **Disallowed costs**. When you are writing your grant application, you try to think of everything you'll need to implement your project. However, once the grant has been awarded and the funds are available to draw down, the person in charge of organizational finances may become busy and forget to check expense receipts or requested equipment or materials purchases to determine if they were initially included in the application's project budget. Approving a new expense that was never mentioned in the grant application or agreed on at the signing of the grant contract or agreement can result in a disallowed cost. If the federal government rejects your expenditures because they violate federal cost principles, will your organization have reserve funds to pay for the items needed for the project, but not covered by the grant funds?

Strings Attached to Foundation, Corporate Grants

Foundation Subcontracting Requirements. Some community foundations will require a grantee to subcontract some of its program delivery services to a smaller nonprofit organization that may have failed to receive a grant award. Why would a foundation grantmaker want a grantee to help an organization that failed to receive a grant? Because the foundation's motive is to build the capacity of the organization that did not meet their funding guidelines. This request can often happen in both small- and large-scale communities. If this happens to your organization, you may be asked to meet with the foundation's program officer to discuss resubmitting your project description to include the unsuccessful applicant. In fact, this request might even be a condition of your organization receiving its grant.

Corporate Product Marketing. Some corporate grantmakers will request permission to use your name or your organization's name in its marketing. Others may restrict you to using only their products. For example, your organization proposes a project to serve the elderly that includes teaching them basic hygiene practices when they have limited mobility. If you were awarded a grant by a corporation that just happened to manufacture a brand name deodorant, they might require that you hand out their products to all participants or steer them toward purchasing their products. Before you agree to any "strings," make sure that they comply with your local laws and your organization's regulations.

Expect Accountability at a Different Level. While most foundation and corporate grantmakers don't have the rigorous assurances and certifications requirements of federal agencies, they will expect your organization to have 100 percent accountability in all financial and program-related reporting. Small- to mid-size foundations may award your organization 100 percent of the grant monies requested upfront. Larger foundations usually advance monies on a quarterly or twice yearly schedule.

Important Steps to Take Before Looking for Grant Funding

Step 1: Clearly define the goal of the initiative for which your organization seeks grant support. How can you randomly look for grant funding opportunities if you don't have a clear goal statement of the project's purpose?

Step 2: Set aside time to have a pre-planning meeting with your organization's key staff to discuss how much effort and human resources can be committed to the project. Remember, not every expense can be charged to the grant's project budget. Your organization will need to have the internal capacity to commit its own in-kind effort.

Step 3: Determine if your organization has the financial ability to meet any matching requirements of the grantmaking agency. Are the funds needed to meet the match already on deposit? Will you need to request the funds from a private sector grantmaker? Will the private sector grantmaker be making a funding decision in time to meet the cash match requirements of the federal grantmaking agency?

Step 4: Prepare a draft budget to estimate how much funding you'll need from a grant award to implement the project the way you envision it. If your goal for the funding is large scale and your draft budget adds up to $400,000, you'll need to look for grant funding that has an award amount of at least $400,000.

Step 5: Take a long and hard look at the turnover rate among your organization's administrators. What will happen if the grant is funded under one administration and they leave six months into Year 1 of a three-year grant award? Who on the new team will be able to come in and quickly orient themselves to the grantmaker's reporting and project implementation requirements? Will the grant award be returned because no one in the new administration was aware that grant monies were awarded? If your organization does not have the track record or internal capacity to manage a federal grant award, then look for other types of grantmakers, such as foundations, corporations and state agencies.

Getting Help With the Grantseeking and Writing Processes

Are you already wearing too many hats at your organization and the new duties just keep coming? Most full-time administrators and employees feel overworked and overwhelmed – daily. Have you considered contracting with a grant professional?

There are many types of grant professionals that provide services to nonprofit organizations and for-profit corporations. Services available include:

- conducting funding needs assessments;

- conducting funding searches;

- facilitating project planning meetings;

- identifying potential partnering agencies;

- attending grantmaker technical assistance workshops;

- researching best practices for inclusion in the program design narrative;

- identifying third-party evaluators for your projects;

- writing part or all of the grant application;

- preparing financial projections for multi-year project budget summaries;

- coordinating your grant management process once your organization has received a grant award; and

- conducting grant writing workshops for your staff.

Finding Funds to Hire a Grant Professional. If your organization finds itself in need of assistance from a grant professional, you'll first need to identify how you're going to pay for the consultant's services. The ideal scenario would be that your organization has discretionary funds to contract with a grant professional. Grant consultants cannot be paid with grant funds for services that were completed prior to the official grant award announcement date. Simply stated: You can't use new monies to pay old bills. Doing so could cause your organization to have to repay this disallowed cost and possibly forfeit your entire grant award.

Community foundations will often provide funds needed to hire a qualified grant professional. Local bank foundations and bank trustees who have managed private philanthropic funds might be other sources of funding, too. The rule here is if you don't have the funds to hire a grant professional, let everyone know, from your board members to your volunteers to the local Chamber of Commerce, to your banker or any anyone else that has the financial resources to help your organization. If you don't ask, you don't receive. This is the mantra in all types of grantseeking and fundraising.

One final thought on how to hire a grant professional. Talk to your human resources manager to see if there are any unfilled positions that have been funded but remain vacant. Often, the services of a grant professional can be secured through a virtual employment contract. This means they are paid a part-time or full-time salary to write a negotiated number of projects per year. The consultant works out of their own office with their own equipment and other resources. This individual or firm can be local or in another state. With today's communications technologies, it's possible to provide all of the needed services from a distance.

©Thompson Publishing Group

How to Work with a Grant Professional. I found some timely tips on how to work with a grant professional on the SchoolGrants.org Web site. I think these tips apply to any type of grant professional.

HIRING A GRANT WRITING CONSULTANT

Some schools, local governments and nonprofit organizations turn to professional grant writers to assist them in writing proposals. This is often a good solution since grant seeking is a time-consuming process and requires special skills.

There are several very important considerations when seeking outside assistance with grant-writing:

- The job of a consultant grant writer is to **assist** those who are seeking the grant. Do not fall prey to the temptation of allowing the grant writer to plan, design and write your proposal for you. This will result in a project that the grant writer supports but that may not be something you and your staff can or want to do.

- Hiring or relying on an outside grant writer should not relieve the group that wants the grant of devoting time to planning a project and overseeing the design and writing of a proposal.

- Do not allow the consultant to put requirements into a proposal because "you always do this" or "all grants require this component." If required by the grant or desired by your organization include the component. If outside your goals and objectives, ascertain for yourself if it is a required element in the particular grant for which you are applying.

- Do not hire a consultant who does not insist on planning meetings with you and your staff. It is vital to the success of the future project that all stakeholders have input into the project being designed.

- Do not expect a consultant to write a winning proposal overnight. The time between learning of a grant opportunity and the application deadline is often tight but allow as much time as possible for preparation of the proposal.

- Review drafts of the proposal and do not hesitate to question what you read in the draft. The consultant works for you – the project that is designed must be **your** project.

- Remember that, while writing proposals is time-consuming, running projects is much more so. If you do not have time to devote to the initial stages – planning and overseeing the design of a grant proposal – you may not have time to run the project if the proposal is successful.

- Remember that grant writing consultants are professionals and skilled in the grant writing business. Most consultants will require an hourly fee to write your proposal just as doctors, attorneys and accountants charge for their expertise. The costs of obtaining a grant are unallowable.

- Save money by assisting the grant writer in every way possible. It may be helpful to bring the consultant in at the very beginning to describe his or her needs for proposal development. Devote staff time to gathering and developing the information while the consultant is "off the clock."

- No grant writer is successful all the time. Avoid using any consultant who guarantees a successful proposal.

Adapted from Schoolgrants.org. Reprinted with permission.

How Grantmakers View the Use of Grant Professionals. Federal grantmaking agencies do not care if you write your own grant application or work with a grant professional. Nor do foundation and corporate grantmakers. Foundation and corporate givers do, however, like to have some type of communication take place between the grant applicant's contact person and their program officers prior to submitting the grant proposal for consideration. Once your grant professional identifies private sector funding sources for your organization's project ideas, you need to designate a contact person to communicate with the grantmaker's program staff.

Finding Grant Professionals. There are several professional organizations for grant professionals. The top two are the American Association of Grant Professionals and the Association of American Fundraising Professionals. Both groups have a consultant's directory on their Web sites.

- **Grantprofessionals.org** – The American Association of Grant Professionals (AAGP) builds and supports an international community of grant professionals (more than 900 members) committed to serving the greater public good by practicing the highest ethical and professional standards.

- **NSFRE.org** - The Association of Fundraising Professionals (AFP) represents 26,000 members in 172 chapters throughout the United States, Canada, Mexico and China working to advance philanthropy through advocacy, research, education and certification programs.

Creating a Grant Proposal Library

Another way to prepare yourself and your organization for the grantseeking process it to create a grant proposal library, a collection of successfully funded grant proposals. Requesting copies of funded proposals from grantmakers and grantees is common practice among successful grant writers. The intent of your request is not to copy winning language word for word or to plagiarize someone else's hard research. The intent is to acquire outstanding examples of winning formats, graphics, best practices, management plans, evaluation methodologies and all of the other good parts of the proposal package. I've saved to my Web browser for repeated visits and to download updates a number of Web sites that offer proposal examples. Here are the top Web sites for finding proposal examples to add to your electronic (saved files) or hard copy grant proposal library. **Note:** Most of the proposal examples are free; some must be purchased and come in spiral-bound book format or on CDs.

Resource: The Foundation Center
Content: The Foundation Center's Guide to Winning Proposals and Guide to Winning Proposals II. This book includes actual cover letters, letters of inquiry, budgets and vital supplementary documents needed to develop a complete proposal. The site features grant proposals that have been funded by some of today's most influential grantmakers. Each proposal – reprinted in its entirety – includes commentary by the program officer, executive director or other funding decision maker who awarded that grant. Proposals are included from large and small, local and national organizations, and for many different

support purposes, including basic budgetary support, special projects, construction, staff positions and more.

Web site address: http://fdncenter.org/getstarted/faqs/html/propsample.html
Cost to Access/Download: Yes

Resource: The Grantsmanship Center
Content: The Grantsmanship Center's Library of Winning Grant Proposals consists entirely of recently funded, top-ranked grant proposals in a wide variety of subject areas. All the proposals in this continuously expanding collection have been selected by major government funders from among their highest-rated grant applications. You can select the proposal subject areas from a long list and order customized multi-CD sets.
Web site address: http://www.tgcigrantproposals.com/
Cost to Access/Download: Yes

Resource: SchoolGrants
Content: A large number of successful proposals have been shared with the School-Grants community by organizations across the United States. This Web site has foundation, corporate, state and federal government proposal examples.
Web site address: http://www.k12grants.org/samples/
Cost to Access/Download: No

Resource: U.S. Department of Education
Content: Sample proposals from the U.S. Department of Education: Center for Faith-Based and Community Initiatives
Web site address: http://www.ed.gov/about/inits/list/fbci/grants2.html
Cost to Access/Download: No

Resource: University of Kansas Community Toolbox – Community WorkStation
Content: Examples of completed proposals.
Web site address: http://ctb.ku.edu/tools/writegrantapplication/examples.jsp
Cost to Access/Download: No

In addition to ordering or downloading examples of funded grant proposals from the Web sites listed, you can also contact grant professionals at other organizations and ask them if they will share a copy or two of a funded grant proposal with you and others in your organization involved in the grantseeking and grant writing process. You can also call local foundation and corporate grantmakers to request copies of funded grant proposals. Be open minded about these requests. While they might say no, they can also respond positively. Remember, if you don't ask, you have a zero chance of receiving anything.

Once you've started to collect examples of funded proposals, you'll need to quickly organize them for future reference. How can you organize downloadable files? Create file folders by proposal topics so you can quickly retrieve an example for your current project writing area. If you end up

> No matter how long you have been writing grant proposals, there's always something new to learn. I frequently request copies of funded and unfunded grant proposals along with copies of the peer review comments. These examples will help you build your proposal writing skills. You'll learn how the peer reviewer's view proposal strengths and weaknesses.

with hard copies of funded proposals, create a set of hanging file folders with the subject areas on the tabs. Use a storage box designed for hanging files or hanging file cabinet drawer to store the examples.

When you've started to fill your files, you're on your way to creating your own grant proposal library. Remember, you've asked many others to share their best work with your organization. Make sure to return the favor when one of your grant proposals is funded!

Using the Freedom of Information Act

The Freedom of Information Act (FOIA) gives any person the right to request access to records maintained by a federal agency. This act covers any funded or unfunded grant applications submitted to a federal grantmaking agency. If your organization needs examples of what last year's funded applications look like – before you start to write this year's application – this is definitely the route to pursue. By requesting a copy of a funded application and a failed application, you'll be able to compare the difference in the narrative writing style, content, budget requests and attached supporting documentation.

Some federal grantmaking agencies may provide these documents free and others may charge a nominal fee. Also, the documents might be copied and mailed or e-mailed to you as an attachment.

How do you obtain copies of state and federal grant applications that are not available at any of the other online resources? The process is as easy as writing a letter of request to the specific grantmaking agency. In your letter, you'll need to provide the name of the grantmaking agency's division that awarded the grant, the name of the grant program, and the funding year for the document example requested. I recommend asking for a sample from the most recent federal fiscal year. Make sure to request a copy of the entire grant application package (signed forms, signed certifications, narrative and attachments).

Once the grantmaking agency has received a complete request, it has 20 working days to respond with its determination of whether to grant the request. If information is denied in full or in part, the agency must give the reasons for the denial by this deadline. If granted, it does not have to deliver the applicable documents within the timeframe, but must do so promptly thereafter.

The Committee on Government Reform's "Citizen's Guide on Using the Freedom of Information Act and the Privacy Act of 1974 to Request Government Records" includes a sample FOIA request letter. Here's the link: http://reform.house.gov/UploadedFiles/FOIA%20Report.pdf#page=41.

In addition, the Reporters Committee for Freedom of the Press has a user-friendly letter generator on its Web site. It prompts you to enter all relevant information about your request and drafts the letter for you, then allows you to edit it before saving or printing. You must e-mail or mail it yourself. Here's the link: http://www.rcfp.org/foi_letter/generate.php.

 ©Thompson Publishing Group

Navigating the Online Federal Grants Process

3

When I first found out that electronic grant applications were surfacing on both private and public sector grantmaker Web sites, I panicked. I felt very hesitant to trust online registration processes, information field entries or application uploading. After teaching myself the entire Grants.gov registration and submission process, I've gained confidence in the federal government's electronic grant application system. The purpose of this chapter is to help you navigate the online federal grants process.

Grants.gov – Portal for Grant Applications

Grants.gov was created in 2002 to allow applicants for federal grants to apply for and manage grant funds online through a common Web site, simplifying grants management and eliminating redundancies. The first stage of Grants.gov was a successful pilot that enabled participating federal agencies to post and grantseekers to search for grant opportunities. The second stage of Grants.gov was a pilot of the "Apply for Grants" feature, which included participants from 20 of the 26 federal grantmaking agencies, and over 100 grant applicants. Input gathered during the pilot guided further refinement of the "Apply for Grants" feature. Here are some historical milestones for Grants.gov:

- By September 2004, Grants.gov had received 1,000 electronic grant applications.

- By December 2005, Grants.gov had processed 15,000 electronic grant applications.

- By May 2006, Grants.gov had received 45,000 electronic grant applications.

Today, the Grants.gov "Apply for Grants" feature includes a simple, unified application to enable applicants to apply for grants online. The site, managed by the U.S. Department of Health and Human Services (HHS), is a free Web site that centralizes grant information and electronic submission for more than 1,000 grant programs across the federal government. Increasing usage of Grants.gov signals an accelerated adoption of a more efficient mode of grants processing, moving from an 80 percent paper-based grants management process to a goal of a seamless 100 percent electronic environment for the federal grants community.

Registering with Grants.gov

Your agency must register to create a Grants.gov account and wait for approval before you can submit grant applications. Here's a shot of how the **Get Registered** page looks:

FIG 3-1

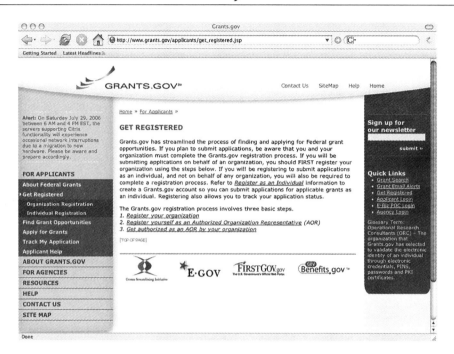

Registering your agency as an e-business point of contact is a one-time process, but it takes one to two days to complete. Be sure to use the registration checklists and tools that Grants.gov provides to guide you through the entire process.

E-business points of contact are required to have a DUNS number, register with the Central Contractor Registry (CCR), and authorize their agency's representatives.

Do not wait until the last minute to register for Grants.gov. If you are on deadline for a federal grant application you may not receive your authorization in time to submit your grant application electronically.

Grants.gov does offer an Organization Registration Checklist (Fig. 3-2). You will find it very helpful when trying to determine if you've fulfilled all of the registration requirements.

©Thompson Publishing Group

FIG 3.2

Organization Registration Checklist

The following checklist provides registration guidance for a company, institution, state, local or tribal government, or other type of organization. The registration process is a **one-time** process, which is **required** before representatives of an organization can submit grant application packages electronically through Grants.gov. The registration process can take **one to three weeks** depending on your organization.

Note: If you are a grant applicant, who is submitting a grant application on your own behalf and not on behalf of a company, institution, state, local or tribal government, or other type of organization, refer to the http://www.grants.gov/assets/IndividualRegCheck.pdf. If you apply as an individual to a grant application package designated for organizations, your application will be rejected.

Grants.gov Registration Checklist	What is the purpose of this step?	How long should it take?	Completed?
1. Has my organization identified its DUNS Number? • Ask the grant administrator, chief financial officer, or authorizing official of your organization to identify your DUNS number. • If your organization does not know its DUNS Number, call Dun & Bradstreet at 1-866-705-5711 and follow the automated prompts to find this information.	• The Federal government has adopted the use of DUNS numbers to track of how federal grant money is allocated. • DUNS Numbers identify your organization.	• Same Day. • You will receive DUNS Number information at the conclusion of the phone call.	❑
2. Has my organization registered with the Central Contractor Registry (CCR)? • Ask the grant administrator, chief financial officer, or authorizing official of your organization if your organization has registered with the CCR. • If your organization is not registered, you can apply by phone (1-888-227-2423) or register online at http://www.ccr.gov. CCR has developed a worksheet/checklist (7-page PDF) to help you with the process, which can be accessed at http://www.ccr.gov/CCRRegTemplate.pdf. • When your organization registers with CCR, you will be required to designate an E-Business Point of Contact (E-Business POC). This person will be given a special password called an "M-PIN." This password gives him or her the sole authority to designate which staff members from your organization are allowed to submit applications electronically though Grants.gov. • Staff members from your organization designated to submit applications are called Authorized Organization Representatives (AORs).	• Designating an E-Business Point of Contact safeguards organizations from individuals who may attempt to submit grant application packages without permission. • Registering with the CCR is required for organizations to use Grants.gov.	• 1-3 days to gather the internal organization information and prepare the application. • If your organization already has an Employment Identification Number (EIN) or Taxpayer Identification Number (TIN), then you should allow a minimum of 5 business days to complete the entire CCR registration. If your organization does not have an EIN or TIN, then you should allow two weeks for obtaining the information from IRS when	❑

FIG 3.2 (continued)

Grants.gov Registration Checklist	What is the purpose of this step?	How long should it take?	Completed?
• If your E-Business POC has forgotten the M-PIN password, call 1-888-227-2423.		requesting the EIN or TIN via phone or internet. • The reason for the 1-3 day delay is due to security information that needs to be mailed to the organization.	
3. Have the AORs who officially submit applications on behalf of your organization registered with the Credential Provider to obtain a username and password? • AORs must register with the Credential Provider to obtain their usernames and passwords at https://apply.grants.gov/OrcRegister. They will need to know your organization's DUNS number to complete the process. • After your organization registers with the CCR, AORs must wait one business day before they can obtain their usernames and passwords.	• Receive a username and password to submit applications through Grants.gov. • AOR usernames and passwords serve as "electronic signatures" when your organization submits applications on Grants.gov.	• Same Day. • AORs will receive a username and password when they submit the information.	☐
4. Have the AORs who will officially submit applications on behalf of the organization registered with Grants.gov for an account? • AORs must register with Grants.gov for an account at https://apply.grants.gov/GrantsgovRegister. They will need to enter the username and password they received when they registered with the Credential Provider (obtained in Step 3).	• This creates an account on Grants.gov that allows AORs to submit applications on behalf of the organization and track the status of submitted applications.	• Same Day. • AORs will be registered when they submit the information.	☐
5. Has the E-Business Point of Contact (POC) approved AORs to submit applications on behalf of the organization? • When an AOR registers with Grants.gov, your organization's E-Business POC will receive an e-mail notification. • Your E-Business POC must then log into Grants.gov (using the organization's DUNS number for the username and the "M-PIN" password obtained in Step 2) and approve the AOR, thereby giving him or her permission to submit applications. • When an E-Business POC approves an AOR, Grants.gov will send the AOR a confirmation e-mail. • AORs can also log in to the Applicant home page at http://www.grants.gov/ForApplicants using their username and password (obtained in Step 3) to check if they have been approved.	• Only the E-Business POC can approve AORs. • This allows your organization to authorize specific staff members to submit grants.	• Depends on how long it takes the E-Business POC to log in and approve the AOR. • AORs can also log into Grants.gov to check if they have been approved.	☐

©Thompson Publishing Group

Now let's talk a little bit more about how to obtain a Dun and Bradstreet number, what the Central Contractor Registry is and how to register with it, and how to authorize your agency's representative.

Request a DUNS number. To register with the Central Contractor Registry, a requirement for registering with Grants.gov, your agency will need a Data Universal Number System (DUNS) number. A DUNS number is a unique nine-character identification number provided by the commercial company Dun & Bradstreet (D&B). If your agency does not have a DUNS number, you should ask the chief financial officer, grant administrator, or authorizing official of your agency to register for a DUNS number online via http://dnb.com.

You can obtain a DUNS number online or by calling 866-705-5711.

First, you'll be asked to select your country and then to enter your agency's name, street, city, state, ZIP code and telephone number. The online DUNS application system wants to make sure that your agency does not already have a DUNS number.

When the DUNS system completes it search, if your agency does not have an existing DUNS number you will be given a link (Register for a new DUNS number) and be taken to the screen on the following page (Fig. 3-3).

FIG. 3-3

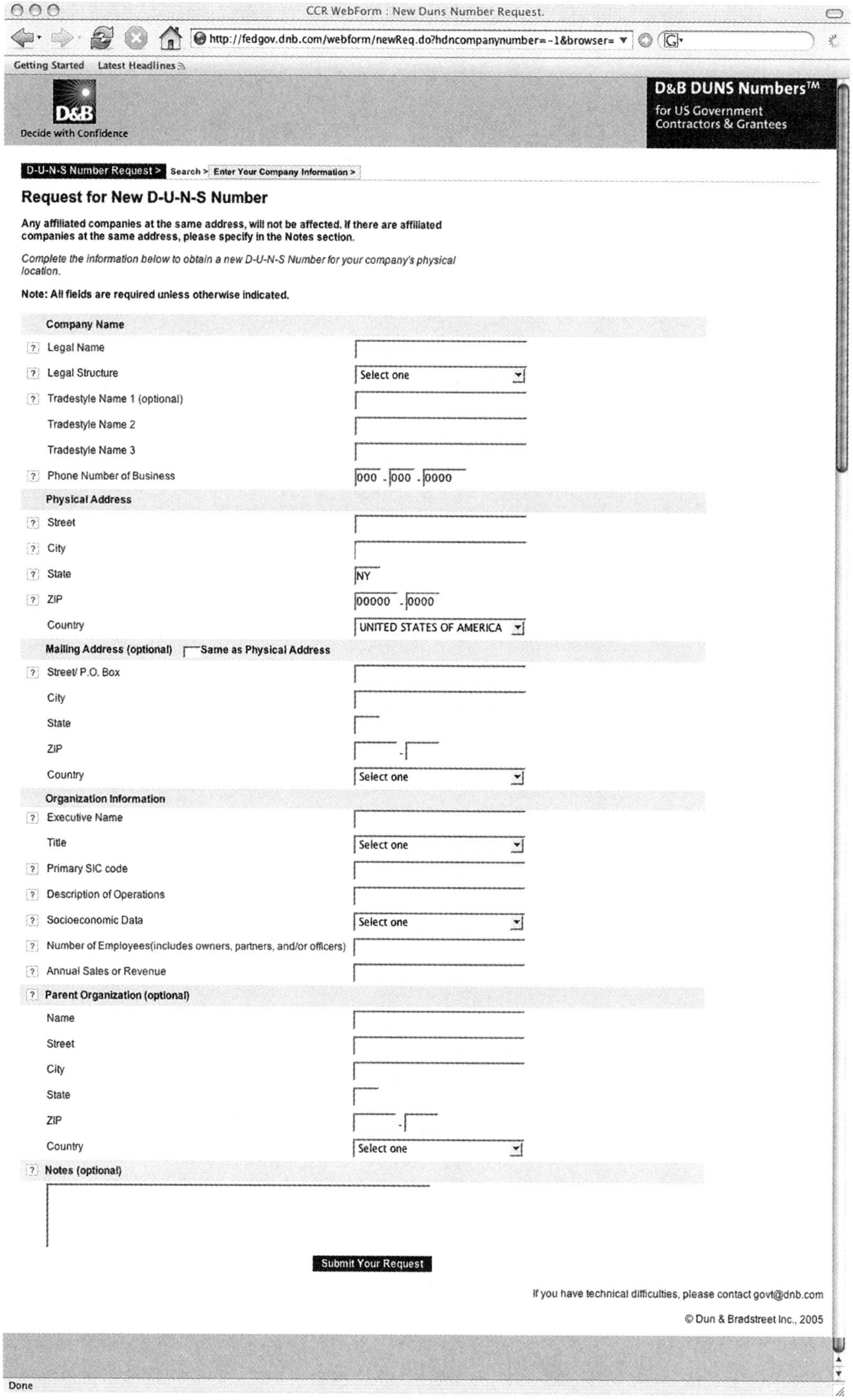

©2006 Dun & Bradstreet Inc. Reprinted with permission.

©Thompson Publishing Group

If you do not enter data into any of the required fields, you'll receive an error message screen. If this happens, click **OK** to start over to enter or correct information. When you are done, click **Submit Your Request**. You will be shown a confirmation screen indicating that your number will be sent to the e-mail address you entered at the beginning of the registration process.

Register With the Central Contractor Registry (CCR). Your agency will also need to be registered with the Central Contractor Registry (CCR) before you can submit a grant application through Grants.gov. When your agency registers with the CCR, you will be required to designate an e-business point of contact. This individual will become the sole person authorized to designate or revoke an individual's ability to submit grant applications on behalf of your agency through Grants.gov. CCR validates applicant information and electronically shares the secure and encrypted data with federal agencies' finance offices to facilitate paperless payments through electronic funds transfer (EFT). The CCR will house your agency information, allowing Grants.gov to use that information to verify your identity. You may register for the CCR by calling the CCR Assistance Center at 888-227-2423 or you may register online at http://www.ccr.gov.

You will not be able to complete your CCR registration until the registry has confirmed your employer identification number (EIN) with the IRS. (It will take 24-48 hours for the IRS to validate your EIN.) According to the IRS, if you do not currently have an EIN and need to apply for one over the phone or Internet, you will be given a tentative EIN, but your EIN may not become active for up to two weeks. If you have questions about your EIN, call 800-829-4933. If you apply for an EIN by mail, confirmation from the IRS can take up to five weeks.

Tips for registering with the CCR:

- Your Central Contractor Registry (CCR) registration must be renewed once a year. Your CCR e-business point of contact should check your renewal status yearly. If you are not sure of your registration status or who your e-business point of contact is, you can search the CCR database.

- Enter data into the fields for the Marketing Partner ID number (MPIN) and e-business point of contact during the CCR registration process. These are mandatory fields that are required when submitting grant applications through Grants.gov.

- The MPIN must have nine digits containing at least one alpha character (this is not case sensitive) and one number (no spaces or special characters permitted). Note: These are mandatory fields that are required when submitting grant applications through Grants.gov.

- Your agency's e-business point of contact will need to know the MPIN within the CCR profile to be able to login to the e-business link on Grants.gov.

- If you have the necessary information ready, online registration will take about 30 minutes to complete, depending on the size and complexity of your agency. If the agency completes the CCR registration process by 6 p.m. EST, the agency representatives will be able to begin the registration process the very next business day.

- The designated e-business point of contact will be notified via e-mail when individuals from their agency register with Grants.gov. This registration constitutes a request to be granted "authorized organization representative (AOR) rights." To assign AOR rights, e-business points of contact should access the e-business link at the top of the page for further direction and guidance.

On the **CCR Welcome** screen (Fig. 3-4), you will be asked to enter your agency's DUNS number and click **Submit** to enter the Web site.

FIG. 3-4

©2006, Central Contractor Registry. Reprinted with permission.

You'll then be taken to a new screen where you'll be asked to enter your agency's name and address. You will then be asked to confirm the information you entered. If you find an error, click **No** and begin the login process again. If your information is correct, click **Yes**.

Next, you'll see a confirmation number screen (Fig. 3-5). Print this screen. You'll need this number to complete your registration process. Once you have printed this page, click **Continue** to complete the registration process.

©Thompson Publishing Group

FIG. 3-5

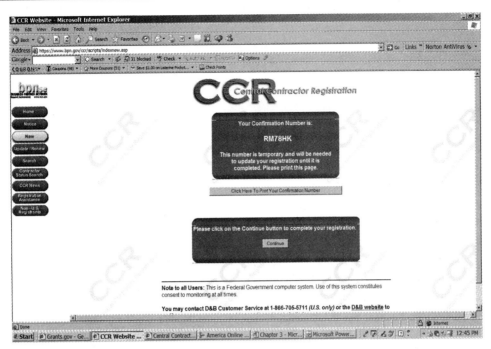

©2006, Central Contractor Registry. Reprinted with permission.

Next, you'll see a screen with these instructions:

In order to complete a minimum registration, enter in a valid value for all of the required data fields, then press the "Validate/Save Data" button located at the bottom of each page to save your data in the CCR system. *(You must do this for each required information page in order to save the data.)* Once you have completed all of the required information pages with 0 errors, the Registration Status box (located at the bottom left of your screen) will say "CCR Update Accepted." At this time you will have completed your registration and may quit or add additional information.

If you quit without completing all required fields with 0 errors, you can return at any time and finish your registration by using your confirmation number. *(The registration will not process until all errors have been corrected, and all mandatory fields have been entered in.)*

Upon successful registration of your trading partner profile (TPP) into CCR, validation will take approximately 24 hours to complete. If approved, you will receive via e-mail or U.S. Postal Service, one letter containing your trading partner profile (TPP) with your CAGE Code and another containing your trading partner identification number (TPIN). At that time your temporary Confirmation Number is no longer valid. Renew or perform future updates and changes by using your DUNS number and TPIN.

The maintenance and accuracy of your TPP is your responsibility. To maintain an active status in CCR and to ensure continued payments on existing contracts, you must renew your registration annually.

Once you have read this statement, click the **Continue** button at the bottom of the screen. You'll now be prompted to enter general information about your agency (Fig. 3-6). Required data fields have a green box with a star in the center preceding the entry field.

FIG. 3-6

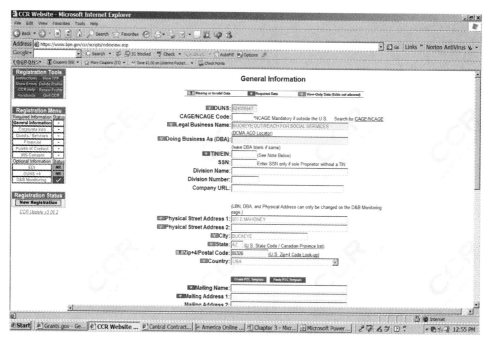

©2006, Central Contractor Registry. Reprinted with permission.

Once you have filled in all the information, click the **Save/Validate Data** button at the bottom of the screen.

Next, you'll receive a feedback screen on the errors in your **General Information** section.

You have three options to choose from:

1. Click **Continue** to go on to the corporate info page;

2. Use the **Registration Menu** on the left of your Web page to pick a specific CCR update page; or

3. Click **Quit** to leave CCR update.

When you click CONTINUE, the **Corporate Information** page will open (Fig. 3-7). Here, you will need to identify whether your organization is a college or university, school district, or other state or local government agency, nonprofit organization, etc. You'll need to fill out this page to continue to the next screen – and eventually complete your CCR process, which will take you two steps closer to completing the Grants.gov registration process.

©Thompson Publishing Group

FIG. 3-7

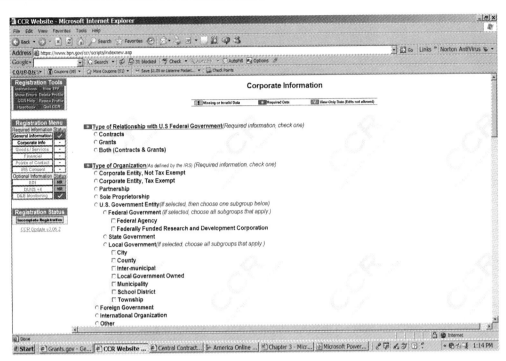

©2006, Central Contractor Registry. Reprinted with permission.

When you've completed this form, click **Save/Validate Data**.

Next, you'll see another feedback screen listing any errors in your **Corporate Information** section.

Remember, if you have errors, go back and make corrections before proceeding. Click **Continue** when you're ready to advance to the next screen, which is the **Goods/Services** page.

Click on this link to find your agency's six-digit North American Industry Classification System Code (NAICS). NAICS six-digit list is located at http://www.census.gov/epcd/naics02/naicod02.htm.

Click on your service area on the top bar and it will take you to a list of codes. For example, if you click "Public Admin…," it will give you a listing of most government agencies.

The **Goods/Services** page will also ask for your agency's four- or eight-numeric digit Standard Industrial Code (SIC). Click on the **SIC code reference** link to find the SIC for your agency. This will take you to the U.S. Department of Labor Web site. On this DOL web page, you will need to enter key words that describe your agency's programs.

Your entries will result in a list of four-digit codes. I entered "Social Services" and Fig. 3-8 is the search result:

Fig. 3-8

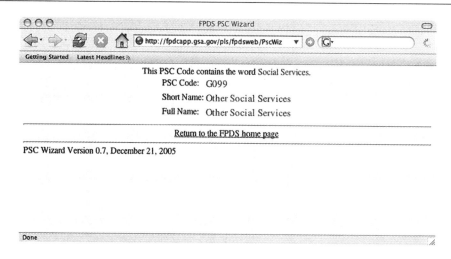

On the **Goods/Services** Web page, you will now be asked for your agency's product service code (PSC). To find your PSC, click on the **PSC Wizard** link.

In steps 1 and 2 your must select from one of the three categories (Research and Development, Services, or Products) and then enter one word or a phrase to search for your agency's service codes. For example, I searched for "Social Services" under the major category, "Services (other than R and D)." In step 3 you must select one PSC category.

Your search results (Fig. 3-9) will be displayed with your product service code.

Fig. 3-9

This PSC Code contains the word Social Services.
PSC Code: G099
Short Name: Other Social Services
Full Name: Other Social Services

Return to the FPDS home page

PSC Wizard Version 0.7, December 21, 2005

©Thompson Publishing Group

Copy your code(s) into the PSC box on the **Goods/Services** electronic form. The last entry field asks for your Federal Supply Classification number. Click on the **FSC Lookup** link to find your agency's codes.

Fig 3-10 shows how my sample **Goods/Services** form looked after entering all of the required codes.

Enter data into this the FSC field only if your agency wants to sell products to the federal government. The FSC is only for looking up product codes. SC is for looking up services codes.

FIG. 3-10

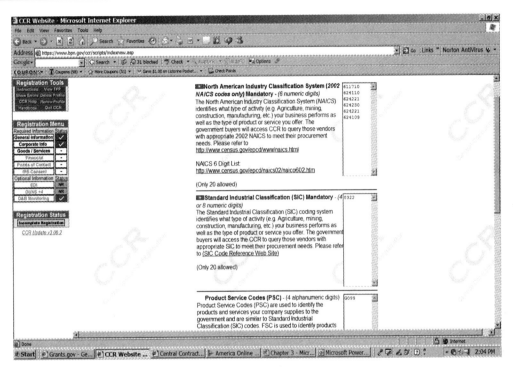

©2006, Central Contractor Registry. Reprinted with permission.

Click **Validate/Save Data** to move to the next screen – the error feedback screen – and click **Continue** to begin entering your agency's financial information.

When you're done entering the information, click **Validate/Save Data**. Remember, if you have errors you'll need to fix them or continue to the next screen until you have entered the missing information or corrected the errors. My screen (Fig. 3-11) shows three errors because I was missing some information on the client's data that I was entering.

FIG 3-11

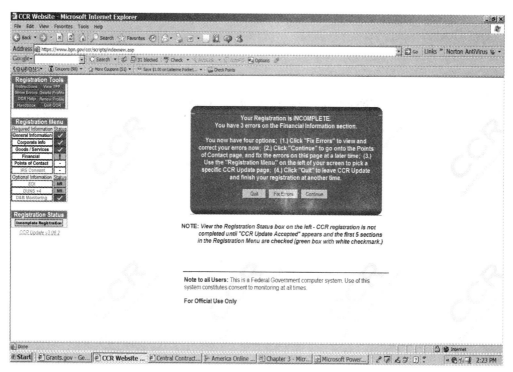

©2006, Central Contractor Registry. Reprinted with permission.

Next, you'll be taken to the points of contact screen where you will be asked to enter your agency's contact person information.

At the bottom of the screen, you'll be asked to create and enter a MPIN number. The number must be nine digits and have at least one alpha and one numeric character. Write the MPIN number down. You'll need it to access the Grants.gov registration process.

Click **Validate/Save Data**. When you receive the error confirmation screen, follow the directions for making corrections or proceeding to the next screen.

The next information screen is the IRS consent form (Fig. 3-12). By completing the information, your agency is authorizing the Internal Revenue Service (IRS) to validate that the legal business name and taxpayer identification number (TIN) (employer identification number or Social Security number) that is provided matches the agency's name.

©Thompson Publishing Group

FIG. 3-12

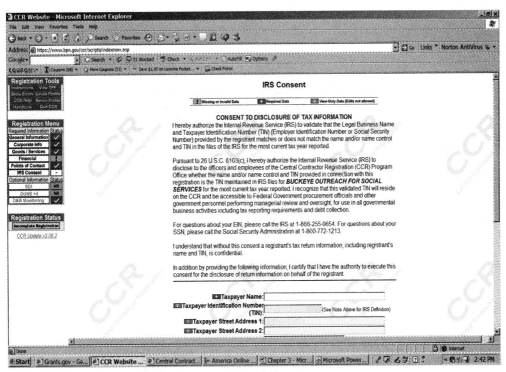

©2006, Central Contractor Registry. Reprinted with permission.

Click **Validate/Save Data**. When you receive the error confirmation screen, follow the directions for making corrections or proceeding to the next screen.

Next, you'll see the EDI Information screen. If your agency is not using a value added network (check with your finance director), you can skip this page. Otherwise, you'll need to obtain the information required for input.

Again, click **Validate/Save Data**. When you receive the error confirmation screen, follow the directions for making corrections or proceeding to the next screen.

The next screen will tell you if you must add DUNS+4 information. For my sample entry, the DUNS+4 number was not required. If the DUNS+4 number is not required in your entry, you will see an "NR" (not required) on the left side of your screen under the **Registration Menu**.

When you've completed and corrected all of your agency's information, you'll be taken to a confirmation screen (Fig. 3-13) indicating you've finished the CCR process.

FIG. 3-13

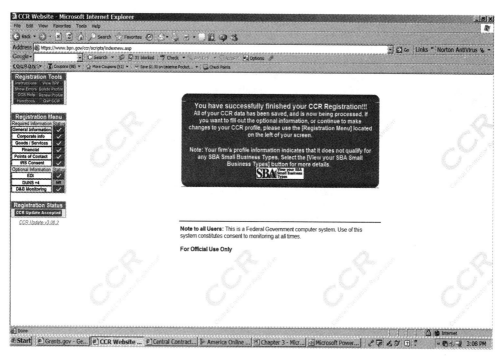

©2006, Central Contractor Registry. Reprinted with permission.

Authorize Your Organization's Representative. You are ready to return to Grants.gov and authorize your organization's representative.

Click on this link to start the authorization: https://apply.grants.gov/OrcRegister.

You'll be taken to the **Register with the Credential Provider** screen.

Tips for registering with the credential provider:

- Ask the grant administrator, chief financial officer or authorizing official of your agency to identify your DUNS number and determine if your agency is registered with the CCR. If your agency does not know its DUNS number, call Dun & Bradstreet at 866-705-5711 and follow the automated prompts to obtain this information. If your agency is not registered with the CCR, the agency can apply by phone (888-227-2423) or online at http://www.ccr.gov.

- Once you are registered, you will receive an ID and password to have your grant application forwarded to the appropriate federal agency safely and securely.

- Grants.gov currently supports only one DUNS number per credential. A future enhancement is planned to provide the ability to assign multiple DUNS numbers to a credential.

- Registering with a credential provider is a simple process. Guidance on this process is included in the tutorial, user guide and help section of the site.Click the **Help** button for assistance.

NOTE: Your agency will need to be registered with the Central Contractor Registry and you will need to have your agency's DUNS number available to complete this process. After your agency registers with the CCR, you must wait three business days before you can obtain a username and password. You cannot register with the credential provider until you have received your CCR username and password. At that time, your DUNS number will be in the Grants.gov database and when you type it in, you'll be allowed to continue the registration process.

When you've received your information, you'll be ready to complete your registration process.

Completing the Registration Process with Grants.gov. You must have completed your credential provider registration and received your user name and password before you can register with Grants.gov. Follow the steps below to register with Grants.gov.

- Click the **Get Registered** link in the left navigation bar of the Grants.gov home page. This will take you to the **Get Registered** screen.

- Under the **Get Started** heading, click the **Register Yourself as an Authorized Organization Representative** (AOR).

- This takes you to the **Register as an AOR** screen. Information about how to get started as an AOR is now displayed. Click **Register With Grants.gov** link on the left navigation bar.

- This takes you to the **Register** screen which displays information about how to register as an AOR. Click **Register With Grants.gov** (Fig. 3-14), which is located in the center of the screen.

FIG 3-14

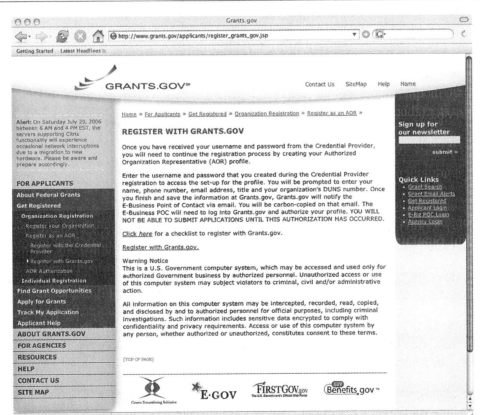

- This will take you to another **Register With Grants.gov** screen. Enter the user name and password that you received from the Credential Provider in the **User name** and **Password** fields. Remember – the password you received from the Credential Provider may contain both upper and lowercase letters. Be sure to enter the exact password you received.

- Click the **Register** button (Fig. 3-15).

FIG 3-15

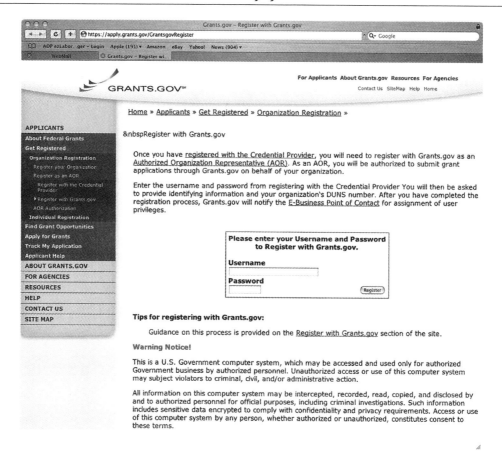

- This will take you to a user profile screen where you will be asked to provide identifying information and your organization's DUNS number:

- Enter your first name in the **First** field.

- Enter your last name in the **Last** field.

- Enter your business telephone number in the **Tel** field.

- Enter your business e-mail address in the **E-mail** field.

- Enter your title in the **Title** field.

©Thompson Publishing Group

- Enter your DUNS number that was entered in the CCR registration in the DUNS or DUNS+4 field.

- Click the **Cancel** button to return to the previous screen.

  OR

- Click the **Submit** button to register with Grants.gov.

After you have registered with Grants.gov, the e-business point of contact listed on your organization's CCR registration will receive a notification stating that you have registered. The e-business point of contact will then need to log into the Ebiz section of Grants.gov and assign the "authorized applicant" role to you.

Note: The e-business point of contact will not be able to log on to the Ebiz section of Grants.gov for the first time until one authorized organization representative has completed the Credential Provider and Grants.gov registration.

Once the e-business point of contact assigns the "authorized applicant" role to you, you will receive an email stating that you have been designated as an authorized organization representative and will be able to submit grants through Grants.gov.

Using Grants.gov to Find Grants

From the Grants.gov home Page, click on **Find Grant Opportunities** in the left navigation bar and then click the link, **Search Opportunities**.

Basic Grants.gov Searches. To perform a basic search for a grant, click on the **Basic Search** link and complete the "Keyword Search," the "Search by Funding Opportunity Number," OR the "Search by CFDA Number" field (Fig. 3-16) and then click the **Search** button.

FIG. 3-16

Examples of keywords: housing, homeless, community development, health, substance abuse prevention, telecommunications, homeland security, and scientific research. Type in your key word and click enter. I typed in "homeland security" and received a listing of 68 possibilities. Here is a portion of my results screen (Fig. 3-17):

FIG. 3-17

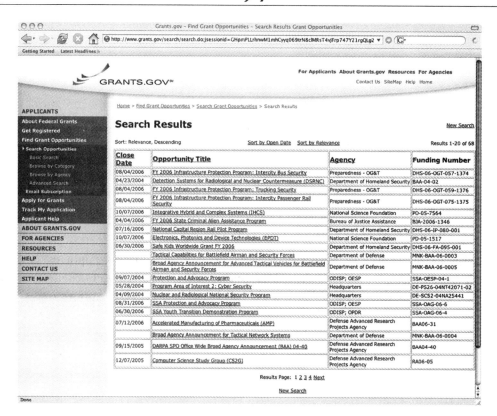

©Thompson Publishing Group

The funding opportunity number is the number assigned by Grants.gov to each announcement. When you click on the funding announcement link, you'll be taken to a summary of the grant opportunity. In the summary (Fig. 3-18), you'll see the funding opportunity number.

FIG. 3-18

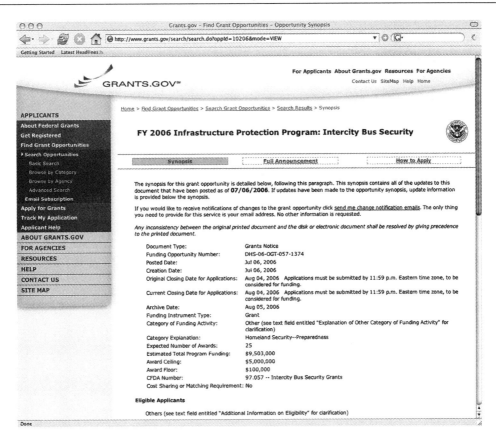

Scroll down the summary to find the CFDA number. It will be a five digit number with a decimal after the first two digits: 97.057.

Advanced Grants.gov Searches. Click on the **Find Grant Opportunities** link in the left navigation bar of the Grants.gov home page to perform an advanced search. Click **Search Opportunities** and then **Advanced Search.** The advanced search screen prompts you to enter keywords. It also asks whether you want to search in **Open Opportunities, Closed Opportunities** and **Archived Opportunities.**

In addition to the keyword search option, you can search by funding opportunity number or CFDA number. You'll also find drop down menus that will allow you to search by **Dates, Funding Activity Category, Funding Instrument Type, Eligibility** and **Agency.** Fig. 3-19 shows you how the top part of this screen will look.

FIG. 3-19

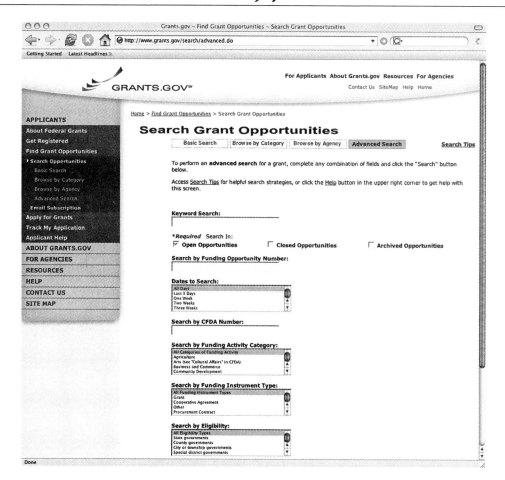

When you search **Dates,** you'll be able to select from grant opportunities announced in the last three days up to those announced eight weeks ago.

When you search by **Funding Activity Category,** you'll be able to search the same kinds of activity terms that I recommended you use when you do a keyword search. The activities are listed in alphabetical order and begin with Agriculture and end with Transportation.

When you search by **Funding Instrument Type,** you'll find that the federal government doesn't just award grants. It also awards cooperative agreements and procurement contracts.

When you search by **Eligibility,** you'll be looking up funding available to certain types of organizations. Eligible types of grant applicants include:

- state governments

- county governments

- city or township governments

- special districts

 ©Thompson Publishing Group

- independent school districts

- public colleges and universities

- native American tribal governments

- nonprofits with 501(c)(3) status

- nonprofits without 501(c)(3) status

- private colleges and universities

- individuals

- for-profit organizations other than small businesses

- small businesses.

When you search by **Agency,** you'll find all of the federal grantmaking and contracting agencies starting with the Appalachian Regional Commission and ending with the Woodrow Wilson Center.

Tip: You can narrow your search further by clicking on the descriptors in **Funding Activity Category**, **Funding Instrument Type** and **Eligibility.** To search across multiple choices in any one drop down menu, after you highlight one search criterion in that window, use your shift key and left click your mouse to highlight multiple categories.

Applying for Grants Through the Grants.gov Site

Apply Step 1: Download a Grant Application Package and Application Instructions
You will need to enter the funding opportunity or CFDA number to access the application package and instructions. If you do not remember the funding opportunity number for the grant, return to the **Find Grant Opportunities** section to locate the grant opportunity and then return to this screen to enter the number. To view application packages and instructions, you will also need to download and install the PureEdge Viewer. This small, free program will allow you to access, complete and submit applications electronically and securely.

For PureEdge Viewer to function properly, your computer must meet the following system requirements:

Windows 98, ME, NT 4.0, 2000, XP
500 Mhz processor
128 MB of RAM
40 MB disk space
Web browser: Internet Explorer 5.01 or higher, Netscape Communicator 4.5 - 4.8,
Netscape 6.1, 6.2, or 7

Downloading and Installation

For users who plan to access, complete and submit applications on Grants.gov, you need to download and install the PureEdge Viewer, which can be accessed at: http://www.grants.gov/PEViewer/ICSViewer602_grants.exe.

For users who have previously accessed, completed and submitted applications on Grants.gov:

There has been an upgrade to the PureEdge Viewer. To upgrade the PureEdge Viewer, access the PureEdge Viewer Upgrade link at: http://www.grants.gov/PEViewer/PureEdgeUpgradeSetup.exe.

Download and Installation Tips:

- You will be prompted to save a file to your computer. Save it. It will download to your computer. Then locate the saved file and open it to install the program by following the directions on the installation screens.

- After completing the installation instructions, you may be asked to restart your computer to complete the installation. When you restart your computer, you will be ready to proceed to the next "Get Started" step.

- If you have a problem installing PureEdge Viewer, it may be because you do not have security permissions to install a new program on your computer. Many organizations have rules about installing new programs. If you have a problem, contact your system administrator.

It will take a while to download.

When the download is done, click **Run**.

At this point, your operating system's Install Wizard will take over.

When you're done, you won't see anything special until you select a grant application to download. In the left navigation bar on your screen, click on **Apply for Grants** and then **Download Grant Application Package and Instructions** and this window (Fig. 3-20) will appear:

©Thompson Publishing Group

FIG. 3-20

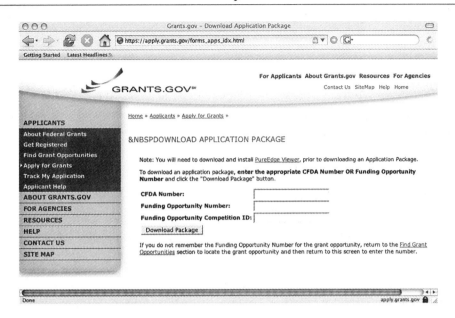

Next, type in one of the following: CFDA number, funding opportunity number or funding opportunity competition ID. I typed in 97.057 for this example. The figure below (Fig. 3-21) shows you how the download access screen will look.

FIG. 3-21

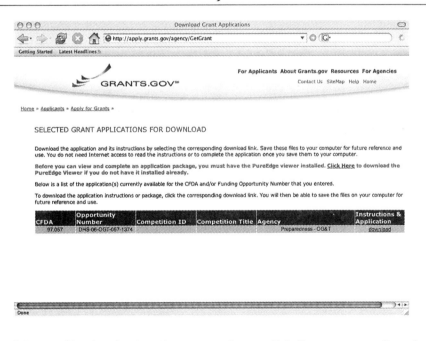

To download the application instructions or package, click the corresponding download link. You will then be able to save the files on your computer for future reference and use.

Next, you'll need to click on **Download Application Instructions** and then. **Download Application** Package. It will take a few minutes for it to download in PureView.

This is your working document screen. You can enter information and select application forms to open and complete online. When you see a square box like the one on the above left of the application filing name box, you can click on it to activate the next area you'll need to type in. Once you start working on the application, you have the options to **Submit, Save, Print, Cancel** or **Check Package for Errors.** You'll see instructions on every screen to help you with the next step.

Apply Step 2: Complete the Selected Grant Application Package

You can complete the application offline, giving you the flexibility to complete the grant application when and where you want. It also enables you to easily route it through your organization for review. Everything you need to know is included in the application package and instructions.

Apply Step 3: Submit a Completed Grant Application Package

To submit the application, you must already be registered and have completed the application package. You will then need to log in to Grants.gov using the username and password you entered when you registered with the Credential Provider to submit the application. You may log in to Grants.gov at: https://apply.grants.gov/ApplicantLoginGetID, or use the "Applicant Login" link in the right navigation bar.

You will be uploading your grant application narrative directly from your word processing files into the Pure-View application system.

NOTE: To submit electronic grant applications, you must be designated as the authorized organization representative. You can easily check your status by logging in to Grants.gov. If you have registered your user name and password with Grants.gov, you will be able to log in. After logging in, click on the **Manage Profile** link. Your status, located below your title, will state: "AOR – request sent" or "AOR – Approved." If your status is "AOR –request sent," you cannot yet submit grant applications. You may correct this by contacting your e-business point of contact. He or she will need to log in by clicking the **POC Login** link in the right navigation bar. They will need your organization's DUNS number and MPIN to approve you as an authorized organization representative.

Apply Step 4: Track the Status of a Completed Grant Application Package

Once you have submitted an application, you can check the status of your application. You can identify your application by CFDA number, funding opportunity number, competition ID or Grants.gov tracking number.

©Thompson Publishing Group

Basics of Good Proposal Writing

4

Every type of grantmaker will have their own instructions for how to write and assemble a grant application package. While some grantmakers might ask for certain documents, others might request only a few of these elements. This chapter discusses all of the possible elements required in a grant proposal, and the types of grantmakers that will likely request each one. Then, I'll give you some brief explanations of the purpose and importance of each element.

Components of a Grant Proposal

Document or Narrative Component	Corporate Grantmaker	Foundation Grantmaker	Government Grantmaker
Cover letter	Yes	Yes	No
Cover forms	Yes	Yes	Yes
Assurances and certifications	No	No	Yes
Lobbying disclosure	No	No	Yes
Budget forms	Yes	Yes	Yes
Abstract or Executive Summary	Yes	Yes	Yes
Statement of Need or Problem Statement	Yes	Yes	Yes
Program design	Yes	Yes	Yes
Management Plan or Key Personnel	Yes	Yes	Yes
Evaluation Plan	Yes	Yes	Yes
Organizational Background, History and Capacity to Manage Grant Funded Programs	Yes	Yes	Yes
Budget Summary and Detail	Yes	Yes	Yes
Attachments	Yes	Yes	Yes

Cover Letter. The cover letter is an introductory letter from your agency's contact person to the grantmaker's contact person to tell them about your agency and why the proposal's topic should be of interest to them. If you've done your homework on the grantmaker, then you know that it's important to propose a project that aligns with their values, mission and funding priorities. Talk about this in the cover letter. The letter should be brief (one to two paragraphs, formal and not a repeat of what you've written in your grant proposal. Always type the cover letter

Private sector grantmakers (corporations and foundations) that have their own customized grant application forms or who accept their state's common grant application form (see Chapter 8) will usually have cover sheets and budget forms for hard copy and electronic grant proposal submissions.

on agency letterhead and have your agency's contact person sign the letter in blue ink. That way, if the grantmaker has to make additional copies of your grant proposal package for their program officers or board of directors, the blue ink will always distinguish the original proposal package. All types of grantmakers want to keep the original proposal package intact and on file.

Abstract or Executive Summary. This is a brief one paragraph overview of your grant proposal. Introduce the project name (yes, name your projects), purpose, goals, objectives and benefits for the target population. Do not exceed 200 words for this section and place it on a page by itself if there are no page limits to the narrative section. If there are limits, type the abstract or executive summary at the top of Page 1 and leave room to start your next narrative section.

Statement of Need. Four words come to mind for this part of the grant proposal narrative section: gloom, doom, drama and trauma. Tell the truth, stick to the facts, support the facts with evidence-based research, and use a lot of community and target population indicators (e.g., risk factors, census statistics, survey findings) to tell the story and establish the base of need for the proposed solution.

Program Design. This part of the narrative section discusses how you plan to solve all of the problems that you identified, or in other words, the solution statement. This section is not complete without:

- a statement on the purpose of the funding;

- your project's mission and goals;

- SMART (specific, measurable, attainable, realistic and timebound) objectives and a logic model table (see the W. K. Kellogg Foundation's Web site for help with the logic model (wkkf.org));

- a listing of community partners and their roles in the project table; and

> If the program design is the solution statement for the problems you identified, make sure that you only identified problems that your agency is prepared to solve with the grant funds. If you listed five negative indicators related to teen pregnancy, out-of-wedlock births, single parents, etc., then your proposed project should be able to reduce the negative indicators. Make sure your program design shows how it will reduce the negative indicators, i.e., solve the problems.

                                                    ©Thompson Publishing Group

- a timeline and personnel/partner responsibility table.

Tip: Write it once, read it three times, fix unclear information, fine tune the goals, tweak the objectives, and use the logic model.

Management Plan or Key Personnel. Some grantmakers only want to see brief experience and responsibility profiles for your project's administrator and other key personnel. However, other grantmakers want to see a management plan flow chart, not merely a few brief narrative paragraphs. The flow chart should show all of the major tasks in your project's implementation process and the one person or workgroup responsible for their implementation. You can use flowchart or spreadsheet software to create an award winning workplan chart.

Evaluation Plan. No money changes hands (moves from the grantor to the grantee) without the recipient (your agency) accepting responsibility for tracking the project's outcomes. The evaluation plan tells the grantmaker who will conduct the evaluation (internal or external designee); if the evaluation plan's design and process includes your project's stakeholders (target population and partners); what you will do if you *discover* your outcomes are not what you planned (you've missed reaching the projected impact on your target population); and who and how you'll share the findings of your evaluation (dissemination). If your agency already works with an outside evaluator, ask them to help you write the evaluation plan for your current grant proposals. Make sure to include funds in the budget (minimum 15 percent of your total project's budget request) for the evaluation process.

Organizational Background, History and Capacity to Manage Grant Funded Programs. Your agency is likely a stranger to the grantmaker you're approaching for funding. In this section of the grant application narrative you must be able to convince this *potential investor* that your agency has been around long enough to manage grant funds, that your agency has the experience and longevity to plan, implement, monitor and evaluate its programs, and that it has the financial management capabilities to develop single audit trail practices. Let them know your agency has been around long enough to know better than to comingle grant funds with other monies.

Budget Summary and Detail. Many grant applicants make the mistake of including a budget summary but not writing the narrative detail to show the grantmaker what's behind each line item entry. Simply stating: "Salaries - $120,000" is insufficient. You must be able to type a narrative for the $120,000 that includes the name of each key person, their job title, that full-time equivalent (1.0 FTE or less) and salary amount. It wouldn't hurt to provide a brief description (again) of their project responsibilities.

Attachments. Some grantmakers will give you a specific list of the attachments they want you to add to grant proposals, while others expect you to know what to include. The standard attachments for private sector grant proposals are:

- copy of your agency's IRS 501(c)(3) letter of nonprofit determination (public schools, colleges and universities, and units of municipal government agencies won't have this IRS designation unless they've incorporated a separate foundation to serve as their grant applicant and fiscal agent);

- copy of your most recent audit or financial statement;

- copies of letters of support (never send originals);

- copies of memoranda of agreement or understanding with partner agencies;

- resumes for key project staff;

- credentials of contracted evaluators;

- specifications for major capital equipment purchases;

- listing of your governing board's membership with community affiliations and demographics for each member;

- newspaper articles spotlighting your agency;

- annual reports;

- copies of evaluation reports for previously funded programs that are relevant to the project for which you're requesting funds; and

- list of all funding sources receiving this specific grant proposal (name of grantmaker, amount requested and status of request).

There are no set standard attachments for public sector (government) grant applications. Always follow the grant application guidelines and instructions for mandatory documents to be attached.

Pre-Proposal Writing Tasks

Here's a checklist for the pre-proposal writing tasks to take into consideration when it comes to earmarking days to actually write your grant proposal.

©Thompson Publishing Group

Project:

Grantmaker:

Application Due Date:

Tasks	Assigned Personnel	Date Task Must Be Completed	Done? [✔]
Internal application guidelines review. Is your agency an eligible grant applicant? Is your agency at a geographical advantage (no recent grant awards from this specific grantmaker have been made in your area)? Are there a sufficient number of grant awards that will be made so that your agency has a genuine chance of winning an award (do not apply to competitions where 10 or fewer grant awards will be made).			
External application guidelines review with partner agencies.			
Contact grantmaker with questions and concerns. Ask to be added to any e-mail alert system for newly posted frequently asked questions or updated guidelines.			
Plan to attend grantmaker technical assistance workshops, meetings and online e-meetings for proposal writing briefings.			
Prepare fact sheet with funding purpose, average grant award, proposed partners, mission, goals and target population outcomes for all partners that will be approached for letters of support or commitment or to sign memoranda of agreement.			
Distribute fact sheet to partners and your agency's governing board and request needed support documents.			
Meet with financial staff to determine if matching funds (cash or in-kind) are available and to request assistance with the grant application budget summary and a detailed narrative.			
Make presentation at the next public meeting of the governing body and obtain a resolution to submit authorization (keep on file in your project folders)			
Funding priority research (best practices).			
Target population research.			
Gather all mandatory attachments for the grant proposal.			
Determine if the writing process will be done by one individual or a team.			
Develop writing timeline.			
Assign writing tasks (writing, graphics, editing, proofing, overall consistency checking).			

First Draft Review Date:

Second Draft Review Date:

Project Finalization Date:

Writing a Successful Grant Proposal – Tips from A to Z

Listed below are tips for writing successful grant proposals gathered from grant writing professionals.

- ❏ Always follow the grantmaker's formatting instructions.
- ❏ Be attentive to all formatting requirements.
- ❏ Choose partners that strengthen your organization's ability to provide the proposed service or program.
- ❏ Do keep staff and board member biographies current – be ready!
- ❏ Evaluate your chances of winning a grant award before you start writing.
- ❏ Find funding sources that have funded projects like yours in the past. Do your homework!
- ❏ Get training in grant writing. It's not a venture of luck, but of skill!
- ❏ Hold partnership meetings to get help with planning and writing.
- ❏ Include your elected officials (for government grant applications) in the entire process – from start to finish!
- ❏ Justify your proposed use of the grant funds with facts, statistics and research citations on similar successful projects.
- ❏ Keep in frequent contact with the grantmaking agency. Attend technical assistance meetings and hand out business cards to all program staff and attendees.
- ❏ Look at online examples as guides for "excellence."
- ❏ Make sure your problem statement is written in clear and detailed language.
- ❏ Never evaluate your own funded projects; always use a third-party evaluator and include the cost for evaluation in the grant application budget.
- ❏ Objectives are where most grant writers make fatal mistakes. Read, practice, review examples and then write clear, measurable outcome objectives.
- ❏ Program designs must include goals, objectives, a timeline of activities and a management plan flow chart. Most grantmakers want to see a logic model.
- ❏ Qualitative and quantitative evaluation measurements are needed.
- ❏ Realistic budget line items must be presented to the grantmaker. Everyone wants a cost-effective project model.
- ❏ Sustainability is a critical issue. Remember to address it in the budget narrative or in the funding agency's specific competitive narrative section for sustainability.
- ❏ Technology is a highly competitive funding area. Make sure you're proposing a state-of-the-art product or service that is not being duplicated elsewhere in the world!
- ❏ Use all available resources to leverage the grant funds you are requesting. A 100 percent match is desirable: $1 in cash or in-kind contributions for every $1 requested from the funding agency.
- ❏ Visualize the funded project; it'll help you write the proposal.
- ❏ Weigh the pros and cons of receiving grant monies. What will be the impact on your organization, employees, cash flow, reserves commitment and other areas?
- ❏ Zenith. This is a zenith project. It will place your skills and organization at the top of the summit. Allocate sufficient time to plan and write the application. Be aggressive and maintain quality communications with your research and development partners. Remember, the next time a funding opportunity is announced one of your partners could very well be the lead agency and offer you a share of the funding award for contracted partnership tasks.

©Thompson Publishing Group

Do's and Don'ts of Writing a Proposal Narrative

Many grant writers approach the narrative of their grant proposal like it's a college thesis or dissertation. Many grant writers fail to understand what a grant peer reviewer looks for when reading a grant application. Here are some do's and don'ts when it comes to writing a winning grant proposal narrative.

Do's

✔ **Cover Letter.** Keep it simple and informal. Write only a few personable paragraphs on your letterhead stationery. Make it personal and incorporate a sentence or two that aligns with the grantmaker's priorities and values.

✔ **Abstract/Executive Summary.** Keep this section to one page or less. Provide an overview of your agency, its partners, the project's purpose, goals, objectives, outcomes and plans for evaluation.

✔ **Statement of Need.** Research the problem. State if the problem is unique or commonly shared by other agencies or in other geographic locales. Use current statistics – no more than five years old unless you're doing decade-to-decade Census comparisons. Validate your statistics with research citations and footnotes or endnotes.

✔ **Program Design.** Write a purpose or mission statement for the funded project. Write global and futuristic goal statements followed by measurable outcome objectives. Include a logic model to incorporate all aspects of project inputs, outputs and outcomes (short-term, mid-term and long-term) into one graphic chart. Include a timeline chart that plots the process objectives (activities), when they will start and stop, and the project staff responsible for implementing the tasks.

✔ **Management Plan or Key Personnel.** Hire or reassign capable project staff that is qualified in the grant funding topic area. Show the full-time equivalent for all staff involved in the project regardless of whether their time will be part of your agency's matching funds or requested from the grant budget. Show who will be responsible for key tasks.

✔ **Evaluation Plan.** Indicate who will conduct the evaluation. Incorporate the four evaluation plan buzz words: qualitative, quantitative, formative and summative. Show how the evaluation findings will be shared with stakeholders and disseminated to other interested parties. Include what will be measured, how it will be measured and what will happen if your agency misses the mark in achieving the proposed measurable objectives for the target population.

✔ **Organizational Background, History and Capacity to Manage Grant Funded Programs.** Write about the background and history of your organization that is relevant to this specific grant project. Include a list of your agency's current programs and their sources of funding. Include any special partnerships, awards or other news that shows the grantmaker your agency is capable and qualified to manage a large grant award.

✔ **Budget Summary and Detail.** Keep your administrative costs at or below the maximum percentage of the total grant funded budget that is allowed by the grantmaker. Check the grantmaker's guidelines for non-allowable costs. Check your calculations. Round up or down on all cost figures. Remember to write your budget summary and narrative detail information using the program design narrative as a guide for what activities will require staff, travel, materials and supplies, printing, equipment, contracted consultants and so forth. Have someone check your calculations and read the program design for possible budget line item omissions.

✔ **Attachments.** Attach everything the grantmaker asks for in the grant application instructions. Minimize attachments (several reduced pages copied onto one 8 ½ x 11 sheet of paper). List attachments in your table of contents (if one is requested).

Don'ts

✗ **Cover Letter.** Don't repeat the application's narrative contents in little mini paragraphs. Don't be too formal.

✗ **Abstract/Executive Summary.** Don't omit this section and don't underestimate its purpose to grant reviewers. Often, the abstract will be the only document read to determine if your program meets the grantmaker's priorities and has beneficial participant outcomes. If the abstract fails to convey the plan for funding, the proposal quickly follows!

✗ **Statement of Need.** Don't use the term "all," be specific in all statistics. Don't use statistics more than five years old. Don't incorporate demographics for the target population that are not relevant to your project's solutions. For example: Your agency is proposing an employment and training project for the underemployed and you write about problems with teen pregnancy, drug abusers and mentally ill persons. Unless your agency is going to reduce teen pregnancies, reduce drug abuse and improve a person's mental stability, don't waste space with non-relevant statistics or demographics!

✗ **Program Design.** Don't ramble. Don't mix your goals and objectives. Goals are not measurable. Objectives are measurable. Don't confuse the three types of objectives. Here's a tutorial: Measurable or outcome objectives are SMART – specific (who will be impacted, where they will be impacted, and how they will be impacted), measurable (increase or decrease by a targeted percentage), attainable (occurs by end of the funding), realistic (don't use 100 percent for any measurement target), and timebound (measurement will occur by a specific date). Process objectives are merely activities (number of people trained, number of workshops held, number of curriculum competencies participants achieved). Impact objectives are all about the benefits to the target population (improved behavior or improved understanding of self responsibility).

✗ **Management Plan or Key Personnel.** Don't omit staff experience and education or their expertise in the grant funding area. Don't omit the time they will devote to the project. Don't forget to include brief descriptions for staff that is yet to be hired.

Don't forget to point out that your project staff reflects the population you propose to serve.

✗ **Evaluation Plan.** Don't evaluate your own projects. Don't omit the contracted evaluation specialist or stakeholder's evaluation team from this narrative. Don't forget you must show how your agency will track the measurable objectives you write in the program design section of the grant application's narrative.

✗ **Organizational Background, History and Capacity to Manage Grant Funded Programs.** Don't copy old boilerplate (previously written narrative from past grant writing efforts). Don't forget that you must prove, in writing, that your agency is qualified and able to manage grants. Don't omit your agency's ISO certification standing if this is applicable. Don't ramble, and don't refer grant reviewers to attached brochures or program fact sheets!

✗ **Budget Summary and Detail.** Don't pad the budget. Don't increase administrative salaries just because it's a grant award. Don't over allocate any staff person to more than 1.0 FTE on all combined grant awards in which the person has been included as project staff. Don't make calculation errors. Don't use odd cents on any budget numbers. Don't omit the narrative detail (lengthy descriptive paragraph for each line item expenditure) and simply prepare a budget summary without supporting language. Don't try to solve your agency's financial problems with one grant request by asking for more than the grantmaker is willing to fund to any one grantee.

✗ **Attachments.** Don't put critical information that belongs in your grant application narrative in the attachments and reference it to the grant reviewer. Don't forget to put all of the attachments in the same order they are referenced in your narrative.

Winning Grants from Private Sector Sources

5

The earlier best known names in private sector philanthropy were Rockefeller and Carnegie, both civic and business leaders. The first structured giving was conducted through newly formed corporate organizational structures governed by boards of directors (an early nemesis of today's 501(c)(3) nonprofit structure held by 21st century private sector grantmakers). When Rockefeller, Carnegie and lesser known philanthropists started their charitable structures, federal income taxes were non-existent. Today's private sector foundations represent significant wealth.

Types of Private Sector Funding Sources

There are three main categories of private sector funders: private foundations, community foundations, and corporate foundations and giving programs.

Private Foundations

A private foundation is a nonprofit organization often founded by individuals or families. Many of these foundations have been created to address a specific target population or to address a specific topic. For example, the Robert Wood Johnson Foundation, one of the largest grantmakers in the United States, focuses its giving on large-scale projects that will improve health care and the health care system. There are three main types of private foundations: the private endowed foundation, the pass-through foundation and the private operating foundation.

Private Endowed Foundation. This type of foundation is the most common. The financial assets for the foundation are used as principal that is then invested. Income from the endowment's investments is then awarded annually to charity. In most cases, only the investment income is spent; the principal (or endowment) is not. Therefore, with sound investments, the endowment can increase in value from year to year to ensure that the foundation has the funds to grow and continue to meet community needs. By law, private foundations must award annual grants and other qualifying distributions equal to at least 5 percent of the fair market value of their assets.

Example: The Women's Fund of New Hampshire is run by a board of directors with the assistance of a small staff. It does not receive any state or federal funding. Private gifts and a growing permanent endowment ensure its continued operation. During its first five years, over 50 organizations throughout New Hampshire shared in more than $190,000 in grants to provide women and girls with opportunities to reach their full potential.

Pass-Through Foundation. This type of foundation is also a private grantmaking organization, but unlike the private endowed foundation, it passes all of the contributions it receives through to grantees. The option to continue as a pass-through foundation is something the foundation's managers can revoke on a year-to-year basis.

Example: The ExxonMobil Foundation, which provides support for social, educational and economic infrastructure in the communities in which it does business, is a pass-through foundation. The foundation generally awards assistance for disaster relief and disease control; contributions to nonprofit organizations; direct spending for community-serving projects; and 'social bonus' projects required under agreements with host governments.

Private Operating Foundation. This type of foundation is typified by a museum, library or historic property that uses most of its annual income to run its own charitable programs or services. In addition to their own operations and services, some private operating foundations make grants to other charitable organizations.

Example: The J. Paul Getty Trust, a private operating foundation that funds and operates ongoing conservation, research, documentation and education in the visual arts, was founded by oil billionaire J. Paul Getty in 1953. The main reason for creating the trust was to establish the J. Paul Getty Museum, which opened to the public in 1954. Over the years, the trust has grown into a multibillion-dollar philanthropic foundation dedicated to enlarging and exhibiting its deceased founder's art collection in the Getty Museum.

Community Foundations

A community foundation is a locally established organization that draws its resources from a variety of donors and contributes funds for a wide array of projects that benefit residents of the community or region. These local grantmakers are a good place to begin your search for private sector funding.

Examples. The Community Foundation of Greater Birmingham, which continually ranks among the top 100 community foundations in the country, was established in 1959 and held more than $125 million in assets in 2004. It makes grants to nonprofit organizations, primarily in the greater Birmingham, Ala., area, including Jefferson, Shelby, St. Clair, Blount and Walker counties.

Corporate Foundations and Corporate Giving Programs

Corporate Foundation. This type of foundation is typically funded by, but legally separate from, its parent company as an independent, tax-exempt entity. Corporate givers tend to make donations to organizations in their operating communities and usually have a specific giving goal in mind. Corporate givers are more likely to support projects that advance their own business goals, such as developing a well-prepared workforce, improving employee morale and attendance, enhancing their image in the community and creating an economic environment in which their operations can flourish.

> **Example:** The Payless ShoeSource Foundation, which supports projects that achieve measurable results in its operating communities, focuses most of its grantmaking efforts on programs to improve the quality of life in the communities where its associates and customers live.

Corporate Giving Program. This type of funding entity does not have an independent endowment. Rather, its funding comes from corporations as part of their annual budget. An advisory committee made up of management staff or the CEO typically direct corporate staff as to where funds should go, or which projects should be funded.

> **Example:** Sempra Energy, a Fortune 500 energy services company in San Diego, Calif., funds programs in education, environment, business and economic development, health and human services and arts and culture. It prefers to fund projects in communities where it does business that will collaborate with others to address issues in the most efficient way.

Giving Patterns for Private Sector Funders

Foundation Grantmakers. Giving by the nation's 68,000 grantmaking foundations reached a new milestone in 2005, according to the Foundation Center's "Foundation Growth and Giving Estimates, 2006." Estimated giving totaled $33.6 billion. This, the Foundation Center says, is up from the previous high of $31.8 billion recorded in 2004. The increase marked the second year of modest growth in foundation giving, following two years of marginal decreases in support.

In 2005, the median change in giving reported by the 853 large and mid-size foundations responding to the Foundation Center's latest "Foundation Giving Forecast Survey" was a 5.3 percent increase. Independent foundations – including family foundations and most of the "new health foundations" that were formed from health care conversions – represented almost 89 percent of foundations and accounted for 73.3 percent of giving. The survey also noted that in 2005, their estimated giving grew 4.4 percent, following a 3.4 percent rise in 2004. This, according to the report, matched the 4.4 percent median increase in 2005 giving reported by the 641 large and mid-size independent foundations responding to the latest "Foundation Giving Forecast Survey."

Community Foundations. Community foundations, according to the Foundation Center's "Foundation Growth and Giving Estimates, 2006," represented only 1 percent of all grantmaking foundations but roughly 9 percent of the giving. In 2005, the report noted, their giving rose an estimated 10.9 percent to $3.2 billion. The median change in 2005 giving reported by the 140 large and mid-size community foundations responding to the Foundation Center's latest "Foundation Giving Forecast Survey" was a 12.3 percent increase. Adjusted for inflation, community foundation giving, when adjusted for inflation, rose 7.2 percent in the latest year.

Corporate Grantmakers. Estimated giving by corporate foundations jumped 5.8 percent in 2005 to $3.6 billion, the Foundation Center's "Foundation Growth and Giving Estimates, 2006" reports. Following a 1-percent drop in 2004, the increase is attributed to gains in the value of existing corporate foundation assets, increases in the level of new gifts into foundations and giving in response to the South Asian tsunami and Gulf Coast hurricanes. The loss of some corporate foundation giving in the wake of corporate mergers, the report noted, modestly diminished the overall increase. The median change in 2005 giving reported by the 72 large and mid-size corporate foundations responding to the Foundation Center's latest "Foundation Giving Forecast Survey" was an increase of 7.1 percent.

Know What Private Sector Grantmakers Expect from Your Agency

Foundation and corporate grantmakers are predictable. There are no secrets. If you do your homework on each grantmaker, you'll know exactly how they want your agency to approach them for grant funding support. Conduct extensive research on a private sector grantmaker using the Internet or by visiting the Foundation Center headquarters (New York City), field office (Atlanta, Cleveland, San Francisco and Washington, D.C.) or cooperating collection site in your state.

Today, in the age of information technology, it's possible to research any grantmaker's background and mission (always look for the **About Us** button on their Web site), funding priorities, how to apply for a grant and previously funded grants. Providing the grantmakers keep their information current, you can glean a lot of information without making a telephone call. By the time you've completed your grantmaker research, you know everything they expect from potential grant applicants.

To find the nearest Foundation Center resource site, go to: www.foundationcenter.org and click on **Locations**.

Here's an example of very clear and concise information from the W. K. Kellogg Foundation (www.wkkf.org).

©Thompson Publishing Group

W. K. KELLOGG FOUNDATION APPLICATION GUIDELINES

How To Apply for a Grant

The Kellogg Foundation is able to fund a small percentage of the requests it currently receives. Many requests are declined, not because they are lacking in merit, but because they do not match the foundation's programming interests or programming guidelines.

The foundation prefers that grant applicants submit their pre-proposals electronically by using the foundation's online application at www.wkkf.org/ApplyOnline. Grant applicants who are not able to apply electronically should submit a pre-proposal document of less than five pages, containing the following information:

Contact Information

- Name (Include Salutation, First and Last Name)
- Title within Organization
- Organization Name
- Street Address
- City/State/ZIP Code/Country
- Phone Number
- E-mail Address

This information should be provided for the representative submitting the request and will be used for correspondence purposes.

Organization Information

- Organization Type – Specify if other than nonprofit organization
- Organization Name – Legal name of organization according to IRS (for U.S.) or IRS equivalent (non-U.S.)
- Other Organization Name
- Tax Status – Does the organization have 501(c)(3) status?
- Tax Identification Number – EIN or equivalent if known
- Year Established
- Staff Size
- Number of Locations
- Organization's Scope of Work – Organizational mission, focus, audience served, and geographic reach.
- Has your organization received previous support from the Kellogg Foundation? If yes, please provide the project number, if known.
- Have you discussed this request with a Kellogg Foundation staff member? If yes, please provide the name of the individual and when and where you contacted them.
- How did you hear about the Kellogg Foundation?

Request Details

- Project Name – Name or title of project.
- Purpose Statement – One-sentence description of what will be accomplished as a result of the project.

- Amount Requested
- Total Project Budget
- Project Overview – A one-paragraph summary of the project.
- Project Goal – Impact to be achieved.
- Project Objectives – Key factors or achievements necessary for success.
- Rationale – Why the project is important at this time.
- Project Activities – Activities that will be performed in order to accomplish the project objectives.
- Anticipated Outcomes – What will be different as the result of this project?
- Sustainability Plan – Ways the grantee, community, or other beneficiary will continue to address the work after Kellogg Foundation funding ends.
- Target Geographic Area – Intended geographic area served by this project. Please note that foundation funding is generally limited to the United States, Latin America and the Caribbean, (for priority geographic areas within this region, please visit our LAC pages on www.wkkf.org) and the southern African countries of Botswana, Lesotho, Malawi, Mozambique, South Africa, Swaziland, and Zimbabwe.
- Collaborating Organizations – Other organizations you are working with on the project and the role of each.
- Project Start Date
- Project End Date
- Other Funding Sources – List all other organizations contributing to the project, including in-kind support.
- Grantee Project ID – List if you have your own ID or reference for the project.

Additional Information

- Relevant information may be included. At this time please do not include: tax documentation, staff or board listings, vitae/resumes, articles or publications, letter of support or photos/music/video clips.

Pre-proposals should be submitted electronically, where possible. If mailed, they should be submitted on standard-size (8 1/2" x 11") lightcolored paper. Please do not provide a plastic-bound, or expensively produced pre-proposal. At this preliminary stage, personal visits to the foundation by prospective grantees are discouraged.

The foundation will give prompt consideration to all pre-proposal submissions. The initial review may take up to three months to complete. If the proposal project falls within the foundation's priorities and available resources, applicants may be asked to develop a more detailed proposal.

Letters should be directed to:

Supervisor of Proposal Processing
W.K. Kellogg Foundation
One Michigan Avenue East
Battle Creek, Mich. 49017-4012
USA

©Thompson Publishing Group

Let's go over what transpires with private sector grantmakers. These are the usual steps you'll take to submit a solicited or unsolicited grant proposal:

Step 1: Search the Web or visit the Foundation Center's headquarters, field offices or cooperating collection sites.

Step 2: Search for potential funding sources for your agency, taking the grantor's funding priorities and grantmaking ranges into account.

Step 3: Isolate several perfect matches for your agency.

Step 4: Visit each potential funder's Web site to find out if you've made a good match.

Step 5: Identify what type of initial contact each grantmaker prefers from grantseekers (letter of inquiry, pre-proposal, letter proposal, concept paper, downloadable funder-specific grant application, common grant application, electronic grant application).

Step 6: Look for grant proposal deadlines.

Step 7: Look for how to apply (hard copy or electronic communications).

Step 8: Call the grantmaker with any outstanding questions or if your agency is near the grantmaker, call and make an appointment to meet with a program officer (take your list of questions to the meeting).

Step 9: Plan, research, write and submit – on time – the grant proposal to the grantmaker for funding consideration.

Step 10: Wait and hope!

Step 11: Celebrate, maybe?

Solicited Proposals. When a grantmaker issues a request for proposals (RFP), it wants to fund a very specific priority area, it has developed a special application to accommodate this special RFP, and it is issuing the call to all interested grant applicants to prepare and submit a solicited proposal by the due date. Here's an example of a request for proposal from the Equipment Leasing and Finance Foundation (http://www.leasefoundation.org/).

The Equipment Leasing and Finance Foundation seeks research proposals for studies outlined below. Right now, the Foundation is accepting proposals monthly by the 15th of each month. Proposals will be reviewed monthly and a response will be submitted to you shortly after each meeting.

Before you submit any proposals to the foundation, please make sure to do the following:

1. Review the Grant Guidelines and Application

2. Search the Web sites of both the foundation and ELAOnline.com for all research and articles currently available on the topic.

3. Contact a staff person if you have any questions.

Source: http://www.leasefoundation.org/

Unsolicited Proposals. While very few federal grantmaking agencies will accept unsolicited grant applications, many foundation and corporate grantmakers accept unsolicited proposals every day. Unsolicited means they publish their general guidelines and wait for proposals to arrive in the mail, via e-mail or e-grant application. Here's an announcement from the Northwest Energy Efficiency Alliance (www.nwalliance.org), a grantmaker that accepts unsolicited proposals anytime.

> Government grantmakers request grant applications by publishing grant funding opportunities at Grants.gov (www.grants.gov to subscribe free) and in the daily Federal Register.

The Northwest Energy Efficiency Alliance has developed this process as a way to identify new projects for assistance by the Alliance. We're looking for fresh, innovative ways to save electric energy in the region. Our goal is to make products and services that use electricity more efficiently available and affordable to consumers and businesses in Idaho, Montana, Oregon and Washington. This portion of our Web site explains the criteria that proposals must meet to be accepted and how to submit your idea.

What is the Unsolicited Proposal Process?

The unsolicited proposal process is one of the ways the alliance develops and funds market transformation projects. There are four phases to the unsolicited proposal process. It is designed to minimize the amount of up-front time that applicants spend to develop proposals.

The initial submission is a response to 10 questions about the proposed project and has a maximum length of six pages. If, after initial review of the proposed project idea application, alliance staff determines that the idea meets the organization's funding criteria, project portfolio goals and has potential to be a successful project, staff and the applicant will continue to develop the proposal through successive review phases.

Each phase digs deeper into the technical and business aspects of the proposed project idea. We anticipate working closely with the applicants after the initial proposed project idea has been accepted to fully develop a project proposal that would ultimately be brought to the alliance board of directors for a funding decision.

Source: Northwest Energy Efficiency Alliance

Common Characteristics of Private Sector Grantmakers

One of the fastest growing grantmaker groups is Grantmakers for Effective Organizations (GEO), with more than 200 members, all of which are major, well known grantmaking agencies. They represent an emerging trend to push grantmakers to rethink their funding strategies, redefine effective grantmaking and revisit how to best meet the needs of nonprofit organizations.

According to GEO, an effective grantmaker has the following characteristics:

- **Mission-directed** – The organization knows what its mission is and directs all its efforts toward achieving that mission.

©Thompson Publishing Group

- **Customer-focused** – Effective organizations are ones that know how to pay attention to what their customers need and respond to those needs.

- **Adaptable** – Effective grantmaking organizations are willing and able to meet changing community needs and adapt to a changing external environment.

- **Entrepreneurial** – Effective grantmakers must look at new ways to fund projects and new strategies to accomplish goals, including the willingness to fund new approaches for solving problems.

- **Outcomes-oriented** – A effective grantmaker is able to define the results it wants to achieve, knows how to evaluate its progress on a regular basis and can use those evaluations to improve outcomes, including making any needed adjustments during a project.

Nonprofit agencies seeking grant funding must also possess these same characteristics if they expect to be funded. If these are the characteristics that grantmakers are aggressively working toward, it is only fair that they expect the same of the grantseekers!

Best Practices for Approaching a Private Sector Grantmaker

Before you approach a foundation or corporate grantmaker, it's important to look internally at your agency. Asking self-guiding questions to reveal internal management weaknesses are critical for demonstrating grant applicant quality management practices, new or expansion program capacity, overall agency capability to manage a grant funded project and sustainability.

If grantmakers are striving to be mission-directed, then your agency can show its successful approach to fulfilling its mission in the community. If grantmakers are examining their own entrepreneurial attitudes, then your agency must show that it has the capacity – with its community partners – to design new approaches to problem solving and expand on proven practices. Finally, and most importantly, if grantmakers are pushing for outcomes-oriented results, you agency must be able to demonstrate its rigorous internal process for monitoring and evaluating existing grant-funded projects as well as proposed grant projects.

What Types of Agencies Do Grantmakers Really Want to Fund?

1. Nonprofit agencies, local governments and other nonprofit entities that run their agencies like for-profit (corporate) businesses.

2. Agencies with high internal quality and fiscal controls.

3. Agencies with track records for planning, implementing, managing and evaluating successful projects and services provided to their constituents.

How Can Your Agency Be All That It Can Be?

Your agency can operate at full speed ahead when it's able to turn itself inside out to find the good, the bad and the ugly. One way to find out more about your grant seeking and grant management abilities is to conduct a SWOT (strengths, weaknesses, opportunities and threats) assessment. If your agency has not conducted an internal SWOT, how will it know what needs fixing and what circumstances could cause it to lay off existing staff or close its doors? A SWOT assessment can help your agency position itself to approach a private sector grantmaker. Let's look closer at what a SWOT is and the kind of information it flushes out.

A SWOT analysis is a strategic planning tool that is used to evaluate the strengths, weaknesses, opportunities and threats of the organization. The results of the SWOT can lead to identifying operating or programming weaknesses that can be strengthened with incoming grant funds. The required first step in SWOT analysis is the definition of the desired end-state or objective. The objective must be explicit and approved by all participants in the process. This first step must be performed carefully because failure to succinctly identify the objective leads to wasted resources and possibly failure of the agency.

> **Example:** A small nonprofit agency wants to apply for funding in response to every grant opportunity announced. The organization has struggled to manage grant awards of less than $100,000 for several years. Without any changes to their internal structure, it might be difficult for the agency to demonstrate to a grantmaker that it has the internal capacity to manage and implement a $500,000 per year grant-funded project. A planning retreat for staff, administrators and board members could flush out the weaknesses and threats to the agency's sustainability and unify the collective group during the strengths and opportunities brainstorming process.

SWOTs are defined as:

Strengths – organizational attributes that are helpful to achieving the objective.

Weaknesses – organizational attributes that will hurt your chances of achieving the objective.

Opportunities – conditions from outside your organization that will help achieve the objective.

Threats – conditions from outside your organization that will inhibit your chances of achieving the objective.

SWOTs must be properly identified since all of the follow-up steps in the process are derived from the SWOTs.

Based on the SWOTs, your organization's decision-makers have to determine whether the objective is attainable. If it is NOT attainable, you will have to select a different objective and begin the process again. If the objective does seem attainable, however, you can use the SWOTs as inputs to come up with possible strategies by asking and answering the following four questions many times:

1. How can we use each strength?

2. How can we stop each weakness?

©Thompson Publishing Group

3. How can we exploit each opportunity?

4. How can we defend against each threat?

One-Time Funding Support. If you find more weaknesses than strengths, then you can engage in communications with potential private sector grantmakers about the results of your agency's SWOT assessment. Note that grantmakers might be cautious about award-ing multi-year grant funds to an agency that has weak internal financial controls, high staff turnover or no previous evaluations for grant-funded projects. If this is the case, then you're better off requesting organizational capacity building grant support. Even if your weaknesses make up a short, fixable list of internal issues, still ask for one-time grant monies. When the agency as a whole has weaknesses, you cannot demonstrate that you're ready and capable of managing and implementing a multi-year grant award.

Multi-Year Funding Support. When your agency has SWOT assessment results that show it's ready to move forward with planning, implementing and evaluating a large-scale new or expansion project, then you've given yourself the green light to proceed with a multi-year funding request. You must still communicate with the grantmaker, upfront, to make sure they're funding applications for initial project implementation and for continuation monies. Examples of large grantmakers that award multi-year grants are: GlaxoSmithKline Foundation, Ford Foundation, Charles Stewart Mott Foundation and the Carnegie Foundation.

Rules for Approaching a Private Sector Grantmaker

1. Make sure your agency is the type of agency a grantmaker wants to fund; if not, find a partner agency who qualifies as an eligible applicant.

2. Be willing to talk and write about your agency's bad and good attributes.

3. Don't omit or gloss over financial audits, reports or statements that show bottom line deficits. Maybe you'll receive a grant award to build your agency's capacity. On the other hand, if your agency has a $5 million reserve, you're going to have a hard time demonstrating need unless you can defend why the reserve should be left intact.

4. Make sure the left hand knows what the right hand is doing – at all times – since private sector grantmakers do not want to receive grant proposals from several different departments at your agency at the same time. Develop a centralized grant seeking approval process.

5. If your agency has not been diligent in conducting rigorous evaluations of previously funded grant projects, tell the next grantmaker that this is the case and that this new grant request will be to bring in a third-party evaluator to examine past project outcomes and prepare a report. Once you have that report in your hands, you can plan, design and implement new programs with higher levels of accountability.

6. Always emphasize the difference or impact the requested grant monies will make on your target population and how your agency's ability to solve a major problem will benefit the grantmaker – your new financial stakeholder and partner.

Private Sector Grantmaking Success Stories

The Challenge Grant Story. During the earlier years of my grant writing business in Michigan, I was contacted by dozens of volunteer fire departments in need of grant funding for pumper trucks or all terrain vehicles. This was well before the U.S. Fire Administration created the Assistance to Firefighters Program. I talked to a lot of grant writing colleagues about approaching some small- to mid-size foundations for these monies, but they said the price for each piece of equipment was too high for most private sector grantmakers.

I spent days at the local library using their Foundation Center directories. Finally, I found a small foundation that listed among its funding priorities: Civic Improvement. Bingo! First, I called the contact person listed for the foundation to discuss their interest in funding equipment. I found out that this grantmaker did not want to fund 100 percent of the equipment's cost, but was willing to issue a challenge grant award for 50 percent of the total cost, with the remaining 50 percent raised from other local grantmakers and individuals.

They had no guidelines, so I wrote a standard proposal format (organizational background and history, statement of need, plan of operation, key personnel, evaluation plan, budget summary and narrative detail) and added 30 letters of support from the community. At that time the pumper truck's cost was $200,000. Within six weeks of receiving the grant proposal, the foundation issued a challenge grant award letter promising the fire department $100,000 if it could meet the challenge within six months of the letter's date. I called the foundation to ask for permission to issue press releases on the challenge grant award. They asked that their name not be included in the release; this was no problem for the fire department.

During the course of the six months allotted for completing the challenge, the fire department was able to raise monies from both corporate and foundation grantmakers. Two days before the challenge was to expire, the fire department was still $10,000 short; it only had $90,000 on deposit. Together, we went live on local radio broadcasts and the only television station's evening news (Friday evening). This last minute appeal resulted

---

WHAT IS A CHALLENGE GRANT?

A challenge grant is not really an exchange of money between the grantor and the grant applicant until the amount challenged has been raised and is on deposit in a bank. The grant applicant must obtain an affidavit from the bank to show the funds are intact and available for the challenge. On receipt of the affidavit, the grantmaker sends the grant applicant a check for the promised amount. This usually occurs 24 to 48 hours after proof of funds on deposit occurs. Some grantmakers will set a deadline for when the grant applicant must have the funds on deposit – if the agency misses the deadline, they lose the challenge grant offer.

©Thompson Publishing Group

in an elderly resident of the community served by the fire department contacting the bank manager on Saturday morning requesting that he drive to her house to pick up the $10,000 she had collected in a glass jar over the years.

The Great Spaghetti Story. A local elementary school district's budget was limited and it was looking for ways to bring in corporate support to help with basic classroom needs. The school officials hired me to train their elementary teachers on how to write corporate letter requests. We worked all day one Saturday on corporate letter writing exercises and how to identify potential corporate grantmakers for cash (grant) and in-kind (donated products or services) support.

The elementary school art teacher was especially eager to locate donations for art supplies. She was also worried about her students' home lives because she knew they went without many basic items, from clothing to food. The school served an economically depressed neighborhood and in many homes, one parent was stretching every dollar just to have one pair of shoes for their child.

When the workshop was over, the teacher sent a letter to a major Fortune 500 corporation that manufactured pasta asking for a donation of several cartons (25-50 small packages) to teach her students spaghetti art (painting raw spaghetti and gluing it on poster board in abstract shapes). Several weeks later, a large semi truck pulled up in front of the district's administrative offices. The driver walked into the central office and asked where he should deliver his load. What load? Five thousand boxes of spaghetti – yes, not 50 small packages, but 5,000 small packages! The art teacher was called to the office to hear this news, along with the superintendent who was in a state of shock and surprise. How does this story end?

The art teacher had lots of spaghetti for the entire school year and the students created wonderful pieces of art for display in the school's halls. What about all of the "extra" spaghetti? The superintendent thought about the many children at his small school district who were using "food" for art, but going to bed hungry each night. So, he talked to a local grocer and was able to get spaghetti sauce, onions, green pepper, paper plates, plastic eating utensils, napkins, punch and cups donated to host a community-wide spaghetti dinner in the school's parking lot. All of the parents and their children showed up on Saturday afternoon for a "free" spaghetti dinner. After the dinner and many gracious thanks from financially struggling parents, the superintendent announced that there was enough spaghetti boxes and sauce donated for each family to take home 50 boxes and 25 jars of sauce.

So let's see, what was gained here? Corporate grantmaker and small business investment, lots of quality artwork experiences, community goodwill toward the school district and families with full stomachs for at least several weeks or months. A little bit can go a long way – it's all in the vision of the grant seeker.

THE CORPORATE LETTER FORMAT
• Date
• Opening Address
• Salutation
• Three bulleted introductory sentences
• Introduce your agency (purpose, mission, programs, services).
• State your problem (2 or 3 paragraphs).
• Beg the issue (gloom, doom, drama, trauma).
• State how your reader can help solve the problem.
• Tell the reader why you chose them, ask for the money, and tell the reader what it will do.
• Say goodbye.
• Sign
• Postscript: One more emotional sentence

Tapping Private Sector Funding To Sustain A Federal Grant

The U. S. Department of Housing and Urban Development (HUD) expects its grantees to find private sector monies to sustain programs that it seeds with federal grants. These stories are about Neighborhood Network Centers that were initially funded by the agency to encourage property owners to establish multiservice community learning centers in HUD insured and assisted properties.

How can Neighborhood Networks Centers open up new revenue sources to fund programs and center operations? By identifying resources among foundations, community organizations and local, state and federal government agencies, and actively approaching them to develop relationships and grant opportunities. Centers successful in obtaining foundation grants generally:

• identify foundations with objectives similar to their own;

• submit applications that demonstrate how the center would advance the foundation's goals; and

• cultivate relationships with foundation staff.

The most successful centers often use a broad funding base, combining funding and in-kind support from federal, state and local governments; community organizations and business partners.

Foundation support was key to both the development and the continuing operation of the Neighborhood Networks Center at Crescent Park Apartments in Richmond, Calif. This center features a large classroom/conference room with satellite and videoconferencing capabilities, office space and a multipurpose room with kitchen and fireplace. Its computer center has 20 networked Pentium III computers, printers, a scanner, Internet access and the capability for distance-learning programs via satellite. Nine foundations provided $600,000 to create this center.

                                    ©Thompson Publishing Group

The Northport/Packers learning centers in Madison, Wis., operated an employment training and placement program, with training provided by the local Madison Area Technical College (MATC). Community Development Block Grant funding through the city of Madison supported the program. After several years, the city stopped funding training programs. The Northport/Packers centers then turned to the Wisconsin Technical College Board System, the public governing and funding parent body of MATC, for support for its employment and adult education and literacy program, which now serves as the basis of the employment-training program.

This partnership solidified a near-perfect match between the Northport and Packers residents' needs and the technical college board's mission. MATC now has an expanded student body, with no need for additional classroom or parking spaces. Moreover, funding for the Northport/Packers learning centers' employment training, adult education and literacy program is now institutionalized as part of the Wisconsin Technical College Board System's three-year funding cycle.

Other Neighborhood Networks Centers have relied on different funding combinations to support programs and operations.

The two stories provided by HUD are excellent examples of agency resourcefulness. All of your agency's funding should not come from one single source. If you create a funding plan that emphasizes multiple funding sources, you gain at every turn or request. Foundations and corporations are the best funding partners to compliment or replace public sector funding.

Winning Grants from Federal Agencies

6

The Federal Appropriations Process

The availability of federal grant funding is the result of federal laws enacted by Congress. Federal appropriations laws include financial allocations for federal grant programs for each federal fiscal year, which begins on Oct. 1.

Both the U.S. Senate and House of Representatives must vote on or approve the 13 appropriations laws and the funds that will be allocated for the grant programs. The president can sign or veto the bills. If an appropriations bill aligns with current presidential priorities it will likely pass and result in a grant funding opportunity announcement. If it doesn't align with the president's priorities it will be vetoed and sent back to Congress for rewriting.

BUDGET PROCESS TIMETABLE

On or before:	Action to be completed:
First Monday in February	President submits his budget
Feb. 15	Congressional Budget Office submits report to Budget Committees.
Not later than six weeks after the President submits budget.	Committees submit views and estimates to Budget Committees.
April 1	Senate Budget Committee reports concurrent resolution on the budget.*
April 15	Congress completes action on the concurrent resolution on the budget.
May 15	Annual appropriation bills may be considered in House.
June 10	House Appropriations Committee reports last annual appropriation bill.
June 15	Congress completes action on reconciliation legislation.
June 30	House completes action on annual appropriation bills.
Oct. 1	Fiscal year begins.

Some federal grantmaking agencies release grant funding opportunity announcements pending the approval of their budget by Congress. When this happens, the peer review and grant making decision processes will not occur until the particular appropriations bill has been signed into law. Others agencies wait until they know their budget has been approved and then write and release grant funding opportunity announcements.

A grant funding opportunity announcement does not just happen. The entire process can take up to one year. You can track the legislative process, including current and past bills in Congress, at this Web site: http://www.gpoaccess.gov/legislative.html.

Timing Federal Grant Funding Applications

Federal officials from 19 of the 26 federal grantmaking agencies have said that most grant funding opportunity announcements are published in the spring and summer every year. You will notice that the number of grant programs announced via your free e-mail alert from Grants.gov will increase significantly during these two seasons.

The best time to apply for any type of monies, including federal, is when your agency is capable and can demonstrate accountability and capacity to the grantmaking agency. Will you see cycles where there are more federal grant funding opportunity announcements than at other times? Yes, but each agency has its only flurry of multiple announcements followed by just one or two per week.

Most federal grantmaking agencies follow the same grant awarding cycles, year after year. This means if you are tracking a federal funding opportunity and you find out you've missed this year's deadline, go to the grantmaking agency's Web site and look at when these monies were announced in previous years. Here's an example of how to estimate when the "next" grant funding announcement will be made for a program from which you are seeking funds:

In 2006, the U.S. Department of Labor released a request for proposal (RFP) under the Workforce Investment Act for Small Grassroots organizations in April with grant applications due in May. In 2005 and 2003, this competition was announced in March with grant applications due in April and in 2004, the announcement was made in April with applications due in May. From this quick research, you can quickly glean that this same grant funding opportunity will likely surface again in the next federal fiscal year in either March or April with grant applications due in April or May. This means you can start tracking the appropriations bill that will fund the program early in the process.

> Winning federal grants involves diligently tracking funding cycles, researching your topic for best practices, making congressional contacts for information on funding priorities, and preparing your application template early for forthcoming competitive grant funding opportunity announcements.

©Thompson Publishing Group

Types of Funding Available from the Federal Government

Most grant writers and their agencies are most familiar with competitive project grants. The federal government also allocates monies for formula grants and earmarked grants. Here's a brief overview of each type of grant program:

- **Project grants** are awarded competitively. Project grants are the most common form of grants awarded by the federal government's 26 grantmaking agencies.

- **Formula or entitlement grants** provide funds as dictated by a law. For example, public school districts receive formula grants based on a dollar amount allocation per pupil. That's why most states have an official attendance account date during the fall annually. Based on the official fourth Friday count (usually in September), state departments of education allocate formula grant monies to each school district.

- **Categorical grants** may be spent only for narrowly defined purposes and recipients often must match a portion of the federal funds. The Head Start Program is funded with categorical grant monies.

- **Block grants** combine categorical grants into a single program. Most grant writers are familiar with the Community Development Block Grant (CDBG) Program. These types of monies are allocated by the federal government to large cities and small communities based on their population sizes and poverty rates. All block grants are considered to be formula grants.

- **Earmark grants** are explicitly specified in appropriations laws. They are not competitively awarded and have become highly controversial because of the heavy involvement of paid political lobbyists used in securing them. Annually, earmarked monies can reach as high as the billions.

How Federal Grantmaking Agencies Solicit Grant Applications

By law, federal grantmaking agencies are required to publish grant funding opportunity announcements in the Federal Register. Either way, these grantmaking agencies must announce to the public that public monies are available through their various grantmaking programs. When you receive a grant funding alert from Grants.gov and you click on the link in your e-mail viewing window, you'll be taken to a **Synopsis** of the Federal Register announcement (see Fig. 6-1). When you click on the **Full Announcement**, you'll see links to download the full Federal Register announcement (see Fig. 6-2).

FIG. 6-1

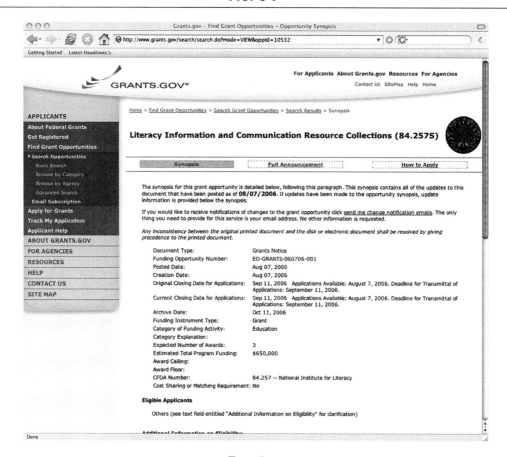

FIG. 6-2

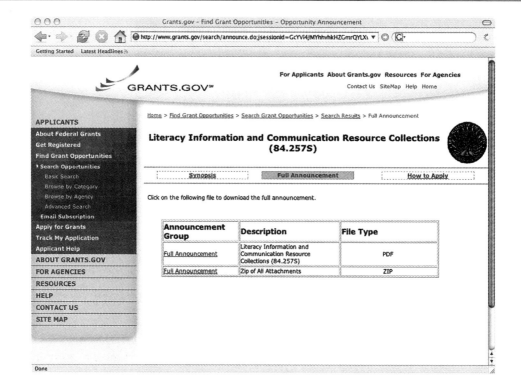

©Thompson Publishing Group

Outfoxing Your Competition in the Federal Grantseeking Arena

Here are some valuable grant writing tips from federal grantmaking agencies and public commissioned entities who know the federal grant award process:

According to a program officer from the U.S. Department of Education, "Your organization's grant application proposal will be evaluated on the extent to which it addresses the selection criteria listed in the grant application notice. Read the selection criteria carefully. In many cases, the criteria will include specific hints as to the type of data to include or specific issues, which should be addressed in order to fully, meet the criteria. Your grant proposal should read like a road map for successfully implementing the project. It should be detailed, clear and concise."

Advice from the Appalachian Regional Commission, "Grant announcements, usually list a contact person – the program officer – who manages the process. Arrange to meet the program officer, preferably in person, or by phone. Program officers are usually experts in the application process and may be knowledgeable about your type of project. Let him/her know about your organization, its accomplishments, and your proposed project. Confirm that your project is eligible for funding. Ask any questions you have about the grant announcement and clarify anything you don't understand. You will not appear foolish by asking a question; however, it would be a real mistake to omit a main item from your grant application."

The Catalog of Federal and Domestic Assistance Web site (www.cfda.gov) has some excellent advice for federal grantseekers: "Ask for suggestions, criticisms, and advice about the proposed project. In many cases, the more agency personnel know about the proposal, the better the chance of support and of an eventual favorable decision. Sometimes it is useful to send the proposal summary to a specific agency official in a separate cover letter, and ask for review and comment at the earliest possible convenience. Always check with the federal agency to determine its preference if this approach is under consideration. If the review is unfavorable and differences cannot be resolved, ask the examining agency (official) to suggest another department or agency which may be interested in the proposal. A personal visit to the agency's regional office or headquarters is also important. A visit not only establishes face-to-face contact, but also may bring out some essential details about the proposal or help secure literature and references from the agency's library. The applicant should carefully study the eligibility requirements for each federal program under consideration (see the Applicant Eligibility section of the catalog program description). The applicant may learn that he or she is required to provide services otherwise unintended such as a service to particular client groups, or involvement of specific institutions. It may necessitate the modification of the original concept in order for the project to be eligible for funding. Questions about eligibility should be discussed with the appropriate program officer."

Grantseekers should also consider becoming a federal grant reader. If you're accepted, you'll be an official peer reviewer (also called a field reader). First, however, I want to share with you how I benefited from taking part in the federal peer review process. Several years ago, I was contracted by a large public school district to write their U.S. Department of Education Bilingual Education grant application. I researched the competition, past funders, and best practices diligently. I thought I was prepared. I wrote the grant application and it was not funded. It missed being funded by 15 points. Most federal grant applications have a total rating score of 100 points. Usually, if a grant application falls below 92 total review points, it does not get funded because of the amount of competition from *really good* grant applications submitted. Before the next funding cycle, I signed up to be a federal peer reviewer for the same competition for which I wrote that grant application (but in a different geographic region from where I lived and my client was located). I attended a five-day peer reading session in Washington, D.C. The entire peer review experience educated me about what the Bilingual Education program officers really wanted to see in highly fundable grant applications. After that experience rating and reviewing exemplary and truly bad grant applications, I used my new found information to write a winning federal grant application two years later.

The Peer Review Process

Reviewers play a significant role in the grant application process. They read and score applications against the selection criteria published in the Federal Register to determine whether the applications meet all of the program requirements.

A qualified peer reviewer is someone who has relevant education, training, or experience in the subject area of the grant competition; exhibits a basic knowledge of common computer functions; has access to the Internet; can successfully complete a Web-based training course; and will commit the time necessary to thoughtfully complete the review on schedule, including participating in the required conference calls.

There are many benefits to serving as a reviewer. Reviewers receive an honorarium for completing their work in its entirety. They also gain valuable insight into the federal grant review process and the methods that each grantmaking agency uses to determine grant awards.

What Do Peer Reviewers Do?

Each reviewer is assigned to a panel to read and score a group of assigned applications. They must thoroughly read official reviewer guidelines, which provide important information on the selection criteria, prior to starting the review. During the review, they will read and evaluate up to 12 applications each, score them, post their scores and comments on a secure online system, and participate in three conference calls over an eight- to 10-day period. Novice reviewers can expect to spend more than three hours each day per competition. Most returning reviewers spend approximately three hours per day throughout the review period. Reviewers also agree to follow the instructions provide by their federal panel monitor.

The federal grant team monitoring the competition then conducts an internal review to assure that the reviewers' scores and comments are correctly completed and relevant.

Section Criteria for Peer Reviewers

Peer reviewers are selected on the basis of their specialized knowledge and/or experience in areas of specific relevance to a grant competition. A peer reviewer is expected to

©Thompson Publishing Group

draw on his or her expertise in evaluating applications according to published selection criteria.

In addition, a reviewer is expected to complete an online training and confirm his or her ability to:

- provide a specific and well-documented evaluation of each application;

- prepare constructive written comments that are clear and easy to understand;

- evaluate applications independently of any personal feelings or knowledge he or she may have about an applicant;

- participate in panel discussions on each application via telephone;

- maintain confidentiality;

- report any conflict of interest; and

- review applications solely on the basis of the selection criteria published in the Federal Register.

> There are a number of peer review models used for federal grant competitions. Examples include a consensus review using teleconference and eMeeting software; an individual, non-consensus review done electronically with no conference calls; a consensus review with the first portion using teleconference and eMeeting software and the second portion requires reviewers and facilitators to be onsite in Washington, D.C., to discuss the applications. The time commitment ranges from 30 hours over a five-day period to 60 hours over a 15-day period.

With the advent of Grants.gov, some agencies are having peer reviewers do their review online via the Grants.gov system. Training in this process is provided by the grantmaking agency and a Help Desk or telephone line is always provided for responding to queries from peer reviewers during the review process.

How to Become a Peer Reviewer

Use an Internet search engine to identify published peer review or field reader opportunities. Here's a sample of what I found when I searched for "Call for Peer Reviewers:"

Preventing Chronic Disease: Call For Peer Reviewers

Call for Peer Reviewers. We are continually looking for suitable reviewers for manuscripts submitted to Preventing Chronic Disease (PCD).

www.cdc.gov/pcd/for_reviewers/call_for_reviewers.htm

Call for Peer Reviewers – Center for Faith-Based and Community

Information to assist faith-based and community organizations in accessing funds from the Department through program grants.

www.ed.gov/about/inits/list/fbci/reviewer.html

EPA: Federal Register: Call for Peer Reviewers

Call for Peer Reviewers and Data on Aquifer Storage and Recovery Wells, Aquifer Recharge Wells, Saline Intrusion Barrier Wells, Subsidence Control Wells, and Aquifer Remediation Injection …

www.epa.gov/fedrgstr/EPA-WATER/1999/January/Day-07

When I typed in "Call for Field Readers," I found these links:

Notice inviting applicants to serve as field readers for the …

Panel discussions with other reviewers will take about five hours and will also be conducted by telephone conference call. Each field reader who is selected …

www.ed.gov/legislation/FedRegister/announcements/2

Field Readers Needed for the Division of High School, Postsecondary …

A request for field readers (peer reviewers) to evaluate grant applications for the Division of High … will be mailed applications and materials, receive orientation by telephone conference …

www.ed.gov/about/offices/list/ovae/pi/hs/fieldread

Advantages of Participating in the Peer Review Process

Participating in the peer review process is advantageous because it allows participants to understand the unwritten expectations of the program officers that will be making the grant funding decisions. The peer review team individually and jointly scores an application. The application is either recommended for funding or not recommended for funding. However, a federal program officer can reverse the decision of a peer review team because more award monies are available than originally anticipated or there is pressure from a senior member of Congress to fund a particular application in their constituency. Remember, if that member of Congress is influential and happens to sit on the appropriations subcommittee with jurisdiction for the grantmaking agency, there might be an extraordinary amount of pressure on the agency to fund the *failed* application.

Once you know how peer review teams operate, think, and score; you'll be a much better grant writer. There are some "funding preferences" that are not written in the grant application's instructions. You must be an insider or have access to the inside (program office personnel) to fully grasp what you'll need to write to win a highly competitive grant application. Signing up for and participating in the federal grant peer review process gives you that inside access to federal program officers' way of thinking.

By participating in the federal grant peer review process, you have exposure to new and innovative ideas in your field and engage in the grant-making process while meeting and networking with other experts in your profession.

 ©Thompson Publishing Group

Case Study: A Winning Federal Grant Application

Recently, I contracted with the Western State College of Colorado to write their U.S. Department of Education Teacher Quality Enhancement grant application. This proposal was for a multi-year, multimillion competition. The college was awarded $4.7 million over five years. First, I want to share some thoughts about why the grant writing process was successful from a grant writer's perspective.

1. The grant applicant had one central contact person who met with faculty and community partners to extract the vision for this grant application and then conveyed that information to an offsite grant writer.

2. The grant applicant was willing to allow a grant writer to take their initial vision (pages of handwritten and partially typed brainstorming notes) and build on it with well-researched best practices for training new and existing teachers.

3. The grant applicant made sure that the central contact person was available 24 hours a day, seven days a week and provide home, mobile, work, and vacation contact numbers so that continual communications were guaranteed between the applicant and the writer.

4. The grant writer provided draft copies, well in advance of the grant application's deadline, for grant applicant review. Not only did the central contact person review the drafts and provide feedback, but copies were given to other key faculty for input as well.

5. At no time did the grant applicant disagree with the grant writer's writing style or research information cited to support the need and program design.

6. The grant writer electronically transmitted the document to the grant applicant who added all of the required forms and signatures, and sent the entire application package to the grantmaking agency.

Before this grant application was ever mailed, both the grant applicant and the grant writer were confident that it would be funded. What we did not know what that the Secretary of Education was so impressed with the grant application that he flew to Colorado to make the ceremonial grant award presentation to the college.

THE COLORADO LEARNING NETWORK PARTNERSHIP
IN RURAL TEACHER EDUCATION
ABSTRACT

Applicant: Western State College of Colorado (Gunnison)

Goal 1: Implement shared governance structure through the development of a partnership Teacher Education Advisory Council.

Outcome: Joint responsibility for the program redesign of the Teacher Education Program (TEP).

Goal 2: Develop a rural comprehensive TEP model.

Outcome: Redesigned TEP (content courses, pedagogy courses, field experiences, alternative program options, professional development, mentoring and induction).

Goal 3: To provide rural local education agencies with highly qualified teachers to fill job openings in high need areas, statewide.

Outcome: Strengthened professional development of beginning and accomplished rural teachers by designing technology-integrated teaching and learning experiential opportunities where research findings can be applied, practiced, tested, and transferred to all rural classrooms.

Goal 4: To strengthen the mentoring and induction programs and professional support between and across school districts enabling the districts to retain higher numbers of qualified beginning and new teachers

Outcome: Changes in P-12 student academic achievement.

Goal 5: To disseminate program "best practices" findings statewide and use this venue to identify new regional business partners willing to share human and financial resources. Outcome: Sustainability beyond federal support.

Model Potential & Population: The partnership's research and trailblazing practices will result in a rural TQE-P model, driven to qualitative excellence by the IBM Reinventing Education Change Toolkit. In Year 1, 50 prospective rural teachers will be identified, trained, inducted and deployed to rural LEAs statewide; 100 teachers will be trained annually in Years 2–5.

Quality of Project Design (Excerpt)

A. The extent of evidence of institution-wide commitment to high-quality teacher preparation that includes significant policy and practice changes supported by key leaders, and which result in permanent changes to ensure that preparing teachers is a central mission of the entire institution of higher education (IHE).

IHE Location and Long-Term Commitment to Quality Teacher Education. This proposal represents the planning and program design work of a regional network of partners whose collective commitment is to improve the quality of new rural teachers, with the ultimate goal of increasing student achievement in Colorado K–12 classrooms in the targeted area. The grant applicant and lead partner is Western State College of Colorado in Gunnison—the oldest Colorado college west of the Continental Divide (hereafter referred to as WSC). In partnership with the Colorado Department of Education (CDE), WSC provides programming statewide, targeting 52 of the state's 63 counties. Colorado Learning Network Partnership in Rural Teacher Education members are located from Denver to the state's most southwestern border (Montezuma County).

The Teacher Education Program (TEP) at WSC has historically been a central mission of the college and was the reason that WSC was founded in 1911. Since its founding, WSC has developed policies and implemented practices to drive continual change and strive for quality improvement in its TEP. Leaders involved in policy and practice implementation include the WSC president, vice president for academic Affairs, and associate vice president for academic affairs; arts and

©Thompson Publishing Group

science department chairs; TEP director; superintendents, principals, and curriculum coordinators; the CDE director of the office of Professional Services and Educator Licensing; IBM; and parents and community members.

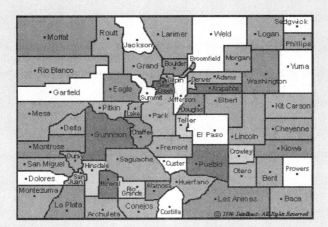

B. The extent to which the partnership creates and sustains collaborative mechanisms to integrate professional and teaching skills, including skills in the use of technology in the classroom, with strong academic content from the arts and sciences.

The Partnership. The long-planned and well-researched vision for the Colorado Learning Network Partnership in Rural Teacher Education is to enhance student achievement in core academic content areas by improving the quality of the current and future teaching forces. The regional partnership is comprised of WSC (TEP and Arts and Science faculties); two high-need Rural Education Agencies–Gunnison Watershed School District RE1J (Gunnison) and Montezuma–Cortez RE-1 (Cortez); the IBM Corporation; and the Colorado Department of Education (CDE). The TEP, which has seven faculty and two staff members, provides pedagogical preparation and preservice clinical experiences for education students. The program also provides outreach services statewide. WSC has 24 tenure track arts and science faculty in the core content areas focused on in this grant application. While the faculty has partnered previously on grant applications and programs with the math and science faculty, they have not had the opportunity to become involved with the Teacher Education Program's activities LEA partners.

The partnership is proposing multiple strands of change to improve teacher education for high-need rural Colorado LEAs, beginning with a research-based pilot in Gunnison and Montezuma counties. The WSC TEP staff worked aggressively for three years to identify and connect with rural partners willing to provide input and share in the vision of preparing teachers capable of providing effective instruction to students with a range of abilities. Every partner is concerned that students and teachers in rural Colorado represent the critical national demographic of being "left behind."

C. The extent of well-designed and extensive pre-service clinical experiences for students, including mentoring and other forms of support, implemented through collaboration between the K–12 and higher education partners.

In 2000, research conducted by Grisham, Laguardia, and Brink showed that eight factors contribute to a quality preservice clinical experience.

Factor 1 – Year-long experience.

Partnership Plan – The Teacher Education Advisory Council will work collaboratively the first year to reform the current TEP. The reform efforts will include improving content area coursework, improving teacher education coursework, and redesigning the 800-hour preservice clinical experience (CDE requires a minimum of 800 hours). WSC's current clinical experience for prospective teachers will be examined closely and the role of the IHE faculty members in mentoring prospective teachers in both content and pedagogy will be strengthened. Preliminary learning community ideas include the partnership's hiring of WSC liaisons at each grade level and/or in each content area. These new liaisons would work closely with WSC faculty members to develop extensive preservice clinical experiences in the targeted LEAs and to develop other forms of support between the K-12 districts and WSC. In addition, because of the insufficient number of qualified licensed teachers in rural high-need LEAs throughout the state of Colorado, the council will begin working on alternative routes to licensure. The Montezuma–Cortez RE-1 LEA will serve as the pilot site for new alternatively licensed teachers who have graduated from the WSC TEP.

D. Whether a well-planned, systematic induction program is established for new teachers to increase their chances of being successful in high-need schools.

High-Need Schools – The Gunnison Watershed RE1J is a rural K–12 LEA with 1,605 students (255 low-income) enrolled in seven schools. It employs 99 teachers. Gunnison partners with WSC for the Campus Preparation Program. At Gunnison, the partnership will focus on grades kindergarten through 12. The Montezuma–Cortez RE-1 is a rural, remote K–12 LEA with 3,091 students (1,667 low-income) enrolled in 13 schools. It employs 231 teachers and serves the largest population of reservation Native Americans in Colorado. At Montezuma–Cortez Middle School, 44 percent of teachers do not have a major, minor, or significant coursework in their main assignment field. Cortez is partnering with WSC for alternative routes to licensure and distance learning communities. In this district, the partnership will focus on intervention methodologies for teachers and students in grades 6 through 12.

Induction Program – In order to receive a standard entry-level teaching license, the state of Colorado requires teachers complete a state board of education approved induction program within their first three years of teaching. New teachers in rural schools in Colorado face some major challenges to completing the induction program. The distances and travel time to urban areas with professional development opportunities are great. Also, there is a lack of veteran teachers within their LEAs to mentor them at specific grade levels and within specific content areas, and those teachers capable of mentoring, often lack time due to expanded responsibilities because the LEA is small and they must perform more than one primary job. This partnership will work with the existing LEA induction programs where mentors are assigned to new teachers. The induction program will consist of ongoing, systematic training and will include a mentoring component. On-site and distance learning communities will also be formed in which new teachers (both beginning teachers and teachers new to the district) network and support one another. On-site support will be delivered through structured mentoring and modeling of effective teaching by successful veteran teachers. Distance support will be delivered through an online learning community that connects teachers from rural schools statewide. The TEP and Arts and Science faculty at WSC will participate in this online learning community. Induction programs will be individualized to meet the needs of the particular LEA; however, all induction programs will focus on research-based effective instructional practices, curriculum alignment, assessment practices, district policies and procedures, and overall culture of the particular school and district. The intent of this induction program is not just to train new teachers throughout their first years but to instill in them the importance of becoming lifelong learners so they will continue to grow professionally throughout their careers.

E. The strength of linkages within the partnership between higher education and high-need schools or school districts so that all partners have important roles in project design, implementation, governance and evaluation.

Key to Stronger Linkages – The Teacher Education Advisory Council will be the governing structure for the Partnership reform efforts. Members of the partnership serving on the council will work collaboratively and be accountable for results-based recommendations. The primary focus of the council will be on learning rather than teaching. Council membership will include

 ©Thompson Publishing Group

representatives from the Arts and Sciences, TEP, and K–12 faculty; K–12 curriculum coordinators; WSC and LEA administrators from Gunnison Watershed RE1J and Montezuma-Cortez RE-1, IBM, CDE, parents and community members. Due to the distance between the members of the partnership, representatives from Montezuma–Cortez RE-1, IBM and CDE will participate in council meetings via Internet video conferencing. The council will meet formally once a month. The core mission of this governing council will be 1) ensuring that students learn, 2) establishing a culture of full partnership collaboration, and 3) focusing on results. As it strengthens the linkages within and among the Partnership in the project design, implementation, governance, and evaluation, the council is looking to ensure that K–16 students learn. The partnership management team will oversee the implementation of this project. The team will consist of a representative from WSC Teacher Education, WSC Arts and Science, Gunnison Watershed RE1J, and Montezuma–Cortez RE-1. Management team representatives will take on a leadership role within the partnership. During the first year of the project, the partnership will work collaboratively to hone the preliminary ideas already generated by the partners. Evaluation data gathered will be used on an ongoing basis to evaluate all aspects of the project design to ensure that K–16 students are achieving.

F. Whether the project design is based on up-to-date knowledge from research and effective practice, especially on how students learn.

The TEP's traditional and alternative initial licensure routes and professional development will prepare prospective teachers to be leaders in curriculum and assessment initiatives. Student learning and instructional pedagogy will include the following research-based effective practices that are proven to improve student achievement:

- Forming learning groups (Johnson and Johnson, 1999).

- Identifying similarities and differences; summarizing and note-taking; reinforcing effort and providing recognition; assigning homework and practice; and representing knowledge (Bogner, McCormick & Fox, 2001).

- Setting objectives and providing feedback; generating and testing hypotheses and cues, questions, and advance organizers (Marzano, Pickering & Pollack, 2001).

- Recognizing that principles of high-quality educational tools accommodate diverse learners by including: 1) big ideas, 2) conspicuous strategies, 3) mediated scaffolding, 4) strategic integration, 5) primed background knowledge, and 6) judicious review (Kame'enui, Carnine, Dixon, Simmons & Coyne, 2002).

- Overlapping all content area instruction with the seven dimensions of literacy: phonemic awareness, phonics, fluency, vocabulary, text comprehension, writing, and motivation instruction (National Reading Panel, 2000).

- Teaching technology as a tool for assessment generation and analysis, concept learning, cooperative learning, diverse instruction, individualization, presenting content and teaching problem solving (Kauchak and Eggen, 2003, pp. 277–278).

- Recognizing that careful planning, different instructional strategies, and classroom management all affect student learning. Using a variety of assessment practices to determine if students are actually learning what they are taught. Also identifying the functions of assessment; developing, administering, and analyzing assessment results; designing alternative assessments, reducing bias in assessment; and using technology to manage and communicate assessment results (Kauchak and Eggen, 2003, p. 396).

Significance of Project Activities

A. How well the project involves promising new strategies or exceptional approaches in the way new teachers are recruited, prepared, and inducted into the teaching profession.

WSC is not proposing TR & S activities.

In several studies, observers rated alternatively and traditionally certified teachers similarly in terms of their performance, particularly when alternatively certified teachers came from structured alternative routes (Lutz & Hutton, 1989; Miller, McKenna, & McKenna, 1998; Sandlin, Young, & Karge, 1992). Additional research (Hutton, Lutz, & Williamson, 1990; Lutz &Hutton, 1989) cites several features that are important to high-quality alternative certification, including:

- high entrance standards,

- extensive mentoring and supervision,

- extensive pedagogical training in instruction, management, curriculum, and working with diverse students,

- frequent and substantial evaluation,

- practice in lesson planning and teaching prior to taking on full responsibility as a teacher, and

- high exit standards.

Identification of New Teachers – The partnership will use two alternative licensure routes to identify teachers with content area knowledge within rural communities across the state of Colorado. Route 1 has been piloted at WSC for one year and is self-funded with student fees. Partnership evaluation findings on Route 1 show that without establishing a new internship component, Route 1's end results are minimal teacher identification in remote, rural areas of Colorado.

Quality of Resources

A. The level of support available to the project, including personnel, equipment, supplies and other resources, is sufficient to ensure a successful project.

All of the partners in this project have sufficient resources to ensure a successful project.

Personnel – All partners will dedicate personnel specifically to implement partnership activities. The personnel will include K–12, arts and science, and teacher education faculty, administrators (state licensing directors, professional development staff, curriculum coordinators, mentoring and induction staff, principals, technology coordinators, administrative staff), and a technical assistance person from IBM.

Facilities, Equipment and Supplies – All partners have adequate facilities to implement grant projects. WSC and both LEAs will contribute equipment and supplies as matching funds to support. WSC will provide a classroom on campus for the K–12 magnet classroom and Gunnison will provide a classroom in the school for WSC student instruction. WSC and the LEA partners will contribute computer services personnel, student computer labs, science and math laboratories, administrators' salaries, existing networking and security software and hardware, facilities use for professional development, prospective teacher instruction and Summer Teacher Institute and research-based instructional materials, and existing professional development, mentoring, and induction programs. IBM will contribute the Change Toolkit and support services, and the Colorado Department of Education, a Web developer and program personnel.

Quality of Management Plan

A. The extent to which the management plan, including the work plan, is designed to achieve goals and objectives of the project, and includes clearly defined activities, responsibilities, timelines, milestones, and measurable outcomes for accomplishing project tasks.

The partnership's management plan will be driven by the mission created by its members and the TQE-P's goals and outcomes.

©Thompson Publishing Group

Mission/Vision: Enhance student achievement in core academic content areas by improving the quality of the current and future teaching forces.

Competitive Preference

IBM Corporation. IBM is a new partner with the CDE, and now with WSC in this TQE-P initiative. IBM lacks a rural school networking opportunity in Colorado that can support the ongoing evaluation of its product designed for educators, the Reinventing Education Change Toolkit. The Toolkit is a dynamic set of Internet-accessible content and collaborative tools that will help educators at partnering LEAs be more effective in implementing substantial, lasting change in their schools. The Toolkit will be used for individual professional development, online project work in content areas, and collaboration among geographically dispersed partners. The fair market value of IBM's donation to the partnership is $100,000. IBM will also provide product support and training, both in person and by teleconference, to new users of the Change Toolkit. The value of support services is $25,000.

Note: You may request a copy of the full grant application and the peer reviewer comments and scoring from the U.S. Department of Education under the Freedom of Information Act.

Why Some Proposals Fail

7

This book is intended to help you write winning grant proposals and boost your agency's financial bottom line. This chapter is about looking at the proposal writing weaknesses that have closed the funding door for some agencies. To gather this intelligence, I've talked to colleagues in the field, examined my own proposal rejections, and even conferred with federal peer reviewers and program officers.

Reasons Why Proposals Are Rejected

Judith Killen, a former Teach For America corps member and middle school humanities teacher developed a list, "20 Reasons Why Proposals Aren't Funded." I read and re-read her list and the advice is on target for any level and type of grant writer. These comments have been gathered from proposal reviews over the last 15 years. They highlight the most common errors proposal writers make in developing and writing their proposals and illustrate by negative example what reviewers look for in "winning" proposals. All of these errors are avoidable. Here's the list:

✗ Deadline for proposal submission was not met.

✗ Guidelines for proposal content, outline and length were not followed exactly. As one federal reviewer stated: "Overall, the most striking reason for low-marked proposals was the consistent failure of universities to be fully responsive to what was asked for in the RFP."

✗ Proposals are not organized so that their distinct sections can be easily matched against the RFP evaluation criteria.

✗ The study or project, although meritorious, was not a priority topic to the sponsoring agency.

✗ Proposed research question, research design and/or research methods were completely traditional. The proposed project offered nothing unusual, intriguing or clever or it seemed to lack significance.

✘ Proposal was not clear in describing one or more elements. Or the proposal was not complete. For example, the proposal did not describe how the project would be managed, how activities would be monitored and results evaluated and reported.

✘ In the literature review or background section, the proposal writer showed he or she did not know the area of his or her subject matter. For example, sources cited were out of date, or the proposal writer overlooked important reference materials or previous studies and projects.

✘ Proposed project appeared beyond the capacity of the individual or institution to carry out.

✘ Method for conducting the research or carrying out the project was not explained or seemed unsuited to the project.

✘ Budget was too high. Budget was too low.

✘ Costs appeared greater than the benefits, or it was unclear who would benefit.

✘ Rationale for choosing a particular approach as the best solution to a research question or problem was missing or not very well thought out.

✘ Constraints most likely to be encountered in carrying out the research were not considered and there were no tactics for overcoming them presented.

✘ Lessons learned from previous projects are not shown or are not made relevant to the proposed project.

✘ The proposed beneficiaries of the project had no role in identifying problems and solutions, in designing the project or in carrying out the activities. Therefore, it seems unlikely that benefits will be sustained.

✘ Work plans are too vague. They lack specifics on what activities are to be done, why, how, when, in what sequence and by whom.

✘ Weak evidence is presented of ability to meet schedules. Detailed monthly or quarterly schedules are missing and timetables for accomplishing work are too optimistic.

✘ Management responsibility and capability are not clearly demonstrated in terms of planning activities, budgeting funds, providing commodities, keeping records and writing reports.

✘ The quality of the writing is poor. The proposal is hard to read, uses sweeping generalizations and jargon, is excessively repetitive and too long.

✘ The proposal contains an unreasonable number of mechanical errors (for example, typos, pages upside down or out of place) showing an inattention to detail and quality of work.

I also received some great insights from Dr. Cindy Grimm from the Department of Computer Science and Engineering at Washington University in St. Louis about why propos-

©Thompson Publishing Group

als are not funded. Here's the list on the most common rejections seen by Dr. Grimm and her colleagues when they apply for National Science Foundation grants (quasi-government organization).

It's already been done.

✗   This usually happens with a proposal where the principal investigator (PI) is new to the field, and just plain missed an entire body of research (possibly because it came under a different name in another field). Usually the review will be a kindly one, and simply say "go look at this work."

✗   It also happens (sadly enough) to new proposal writers because they didn't do a literature search. Please, do your homework.

✗   Sometimes this arises because of a misunderstanding of the proposed research, and a misremembering of what's been done. The best way to combat this is to make sure you've touched on all related research and are explicit about what you're doing that they didn't.

Not enough detail.

✗   This usually arises because the PI hasn't figured out how they're going to proceed. If the reviewers liked the problem area and the approach, then this proposal is a very good candidate for reviewing, rewriting and resubmitting it.

✗   You may argue that if you knew how to do something, you wouldn't be asking for money to do it. Don't confuse not knowing how to do something with not enough detail. For example, I don't know what roads to take to get from St. Louis to New Orleans, but I do know enough to pop-up MapQuest® and get driving directions, and that there's probably a north-south freeway that parallels the Mississippi, and that it will take a day or two to get there.

There's not enough research/nothing new.

✗   This is slightly different than it's already been done. I usually see this with research ideas that have reached the point where most of the things left to do are fairly straight-forward, or just require an application of existing, known techniques. Yes, engineering/follow through is important, but it's not what NSF funds.

✗   There's usually no fixing this sort of proposal. It may, however, make a great start/ first third of your next proposal.

Too ambitious.

✗   I know of several cases where the research in a proposal that got rejected as "too ambitious" was mostly completed in the following year. I think the way to avoid this review is to include at least a few pages of fairly short-term goals that are clearly achievable. Then you can be pretty ambitious in the rest of the proposal.

Lack of evaluation/no application.

✘ This happens if the reviewer thinks you're solving a non-existent problem, or if your proposed solution won't be any better than existing solutions.

✘ If your work is not yet usable in a real-world application, at least come up with compelling test cases and evaluation criteria.

Poorly written.

✘ There are services you can hire that will help you clean up your writing. If you aren't a native speaker, or you don't write well, use them. Most universities have a writing center as well.

✘ Write the proposal early, let it sit and go back to it.

✘ Don't cobble together bits and pieces from papers and expect it to flow.

✘ If you're working with multiple PIs, designate someone as the coordinator and make sure everyone's reading everyone else's part.

This list of fatal errors also comes from Dr. Grimm:

1. Don't spell check.

2. Change formatting halfway through the paper.

3. Use really small text. Don't check your figure numbers and captions.

4. Use equations without defining the variables.

5. Bounce around from subject to subject.

6. Claim you're going to do x then actually describe y.

7. List all of your achievements and describe all of your current research and spend one page describing new work.

8. Define 20 equations without any accompanying text.

9. Make it really difficult to dig out the broader impact, intellectual merit and proposed work.

10. Ask for tons of money for lots of students to do very little work.

11. Assume your reviewer knows your field intimately and jump straight to the details.

12. Cut and paste three existing proposals from different people into one proposal and add a summary page that "glues" the result together.

These are across-the-board *fatal errors* that will **kill** any grant proposal's chances of getting federal funding with any type of grantmaking agency.

If you can avoid all of these fatal errors, then you and your agency likely have a strong

 ©Thompson Publishing Group

chance of winning a grant for nearly every proposal you submit.

Failing and Trying Again

Kitty Pratz, an educator and grant writer from Washington State shared her grant application rejection experience and how she and her writing team used the feedback from the federal peer reviewers to apply a second time and win funding.

Don't forget to use the Freedom of Information Act to request copies of federal peer review or field reader comments. You'll need the name of the grantmaking agency, the name of the program that you applied to for funding, the Catalog of Federal Domestic Assistance number, the grant applicant's name, city, county and state, and if available, the tracking number assigned to your grant application from the Application Control Center. All of the information you need will either be found in the grant application's guidelines or instructions, on your grant application cover sheet (Form 424), and on the return post card, e-mail or letter sent by the Application Control Center to confirm the receipt of your grant application. When filing a FOIA request, remember that most federal agencies charge a fee to cover the costs associated with your request. Be sure to state in your request the maximum amount of money you are willing to spend.

"Our first attempt was not funded and our peer review scores were low. After the initial disappointment, we decided to really go for it and try again. Major credit goes to the director, Tom Christian, who spent nearly a year pulling people and resources together. I spent many hours organizing large amounts of information and writing and rewriting to try to meet all of the requirements stated in the RFP. Our second application was funded for five school districts and was titled: "America's Past Kindles Our Future." It became a reality for three academic years beginning in Fall 2003 and ending in Spring 2006. Many other school districts were interested in the project and so our team wrote a third proposal for 15 combined districts in the center of Washington state. This third proposal was titled: "Teaching Our Past For The Future." The first successful proposal had higher scores than the second successful proposal and we found that confusing as we felt that the second proposal was actually the better presentation. The reviewers were different individuals, of course, and maybe had different expectations."

Kitty was on target with her comment about the peer reviewers. We're going to explore this more in the next section.

The Human Element

As a grant writer for two decades, I can testify about the human factor – for grantseekers and for the grantmaking process. Some errors and resulting decisions are simply out of our (grant writers) control. From foundation and corporate program officers to state and federal peer reviewers or field readers, people will be people. They will have good days and bad days. It is impossible to hit the target every time with every grant decision-maker. As you can see from Kitty's experience, a grant application for the same program with the same program design can be viewed and scored differently depending on the peer review team. Each grant reader has different personalities, values, levels of experience and expertise, and reasons for volunteering or working in the grantmaking field. Those reasons are unknown. As the grant writer, you will not know who's going to read your grant application and decide its fate. You do not know who will instantly dislike your proposal and who will instantly like your proposal. Yes, I already know how frustrating this entire process (peer review) is and I want to tell you that it's frustrating for grant writers and for grant peer reviewers. Every time I participate in the federal peer review process, I am dumbfounded by the differences of opinion among the peer reviewers about each grant application. One likes it; two don't or two want to recommend the application for funding and one is the hard sell hold out that convinces the other two to find more weaknesses and not recommend the application for funding. It's about values, character, ethics, fair play, self-responsibility, negotiation, flexibility and team consensus.

Demonstrating Your Management Capabilities to Peer Reviewers

I talked about this in a previous chapter, but I want to underscore the importance of writing about your agency's organizational and fiscal management capabilities to convince peer review panels and grant program officers that you're ready to take on a grant award and successfully manage a project.

"Capacity" refers to the skills, resources and infrastructure that support the ability of your agency to work effectively. You can strengthen this section of your grant application narratives by checking off each item in the checklist (did you include this information or not). Obviously, you must write to the grantmaker's instructions, but the following information is basic and necessary to show internal grant management abilities.

GRANTS MANAGEMENT CAPACITY CHECKLIST

Information Needed by Grant Reviewer	Did You Include This?	
	Yes	No
Description of your total operating budget (annual amount in dollars) and the source of revenues).		
Description of the type of internal monitoring and audit procedures for grant-funded fiscal expenditures.		
Description of your agency's credit or bond ratings, if applicable.		
Description of fiscal and operational management oversight practices.		
Description of single audit trail practices for all grant-funded programs.		
Description of senior staff members who help set direction and maintain a leadership system.		
Description of agency resources available to support grant-funded projects.		

If you checked "no" to any of the above when you looked at the last grant application your agency submitted to a grantmaker for funding consideration, and your request was not funded, this could be a clue as to why it was rejected.

The Power of Persuasion

As a grant writer, your sole role is to write a grant request that *persuades* the grantmaking agency to award a grant to your agency. Your writing, graphics, page formatting, content, citations, attachments and pre-writing communications work must all be persuasive. The following are some tips on how to incorporate persuasion into the various sections of your grant applications.

©Thompson Publishing Group

Needs Statement Justification

- Write with accuracy and compassion to convince the grantmaker that the need for funding really does exist.

- Support your compelling needs statement with current demographics that are related to the need. Use the numbers to persuade grant application reviewers that your particular situation is dire.

Program Design Sales Pitch

- Open with a purpose statement that tells the grant application reviewers what their monies will fund. Tell it straight and plain to plant the seeds of persuasion.

- Write visionary and futuristic goals that you know you can attain by the end of the funding. Convince the grant application reviewers that your agency has vision and that it will be realized with their funding support.

- Develop measurable outcome objectives that your agency can meet and hopefully exceed during the proposed grant funding period. Convince the grant application reviewers that your agency knows how to develop and monitor benchmarks and that it will issue progress reports on a frequent basis.

- Select management team members and other proposed grant-funded staff that are qualified in education and experience. Persuade grant application reviewers that your agency has the "best" possible management plan in place to succeed.

Evaluation Plan Accountability

- Let the grant application reviewers know who will conduct the evaluation (and provide their credentials) and how the evaluation will be conducted. Convince them that your agency can plan and implement an objective evaluation process (using stakeholders or third parties to validate data).

- Convince the grant application reviewers that there are other agencies around the country that can benefit from your evaluation findings and write about how you will disseminate the findings to peer agencies.

Budget Narrative to Seal the Deal

- Develop a budget (line items) that is modest, realistic and that reflects the most cost-effective program implementation process. Convince the grant application reviewers that your agency has local and regional resources and partners in place already (at the time you write the grant application) who can help you leverage additional dollars.

- Provide lots of detail to account for the activities that every line item in your budget will support (program activities and related expenses). The more detail, the better you can persuade grantmakers that your agency has the fiscal and management capacity to manage a grant funded program.

Forms to Use When Applying for Grants

8

The federal certifications and assurances that need to be included in any federal grant application package were discussed in Chapter 2. In this chapter you'll learn about the standard forms needed to apply for federal grants. I'll also provide you with a list of the common grant application forms used by members of the Regional Association of Grantmakers, foundation, corporate and other private organizations that award grants.

Federal Grant Application Forms

There are several standard forms that must be included in any grant application submitted to a federal agency. However, grantseekers should keep in mind that many programs will ask for additional information and forms such as a project summary and, if applicable, proof of an organization's nonprofit status, as evidenced by an Internal Revenue Service determination letter.

At a minimum, the following standard forms, most of which are reproduced in this section, are required when applying for a federal grant:

- *Application for Federal Assistance* (SF-424);

- *Budget Information – Non-Construction Programs* (SF-424A);

- *Assurances – Non-Construction Programs* (SF-424B);

- *Budget Information – Construction Programs* (SF-424C);

- *Assurances – Construction Programs* (SF-424D);

- *Disclosure of Lobbying Activities* (SF-LLL) (see Chapter 2);

- *Certification Regarding Debarment, Suspension, Ineligibility and Voluntary Exclusion – Lower Tier Covered Transactions* (see Chapter 2); and

- *Certification Regarding Drug-Free Workplace Requirements* (also discussed in Chapter 2).

Grantseekers should check with the federal grantmaking agency and use the forms prescribed when requesting a grant award. An application kit should contain all the correct forms, either adopted wholesale from the OMB or tailored to be agency-specific. As a practical matter, grantees should comply with the specific requirements of grantmaking agencies when submitting application forms. Generally, grant applicants are required to submit the original and two copies of an application.

When completing a standard form, a grant applicant should be sure to write concisely, complete all the information requested as fully and accurately as possible, follow any and all instructions and have someone proofread the form. A grant applicant should include a cover letter, sign the forms and type all of the information in the space provided. It is extremely important that a grantseeker not exceed page counts or space limitations since doing so raises questions about the ability to follow instructions. Each form comes with detailed instructions for filling it out.

For information about filing grant applications electronically, see Chapter 3.

Standard Form 424

Standard Form 424 (see Fig. 8-1) is the cover form for all federal grant applications. Whether you mail a hard copy or fill out your forms on Grants.gov, you'll have to input the same information. This form has detailed instructions on what information is needed in each information field.

©Thompson Publishing Group

FIG. 8-I

OMB Number: 4040-0004

Application for Federal Assistance SF-424	Version 02

* 1. Type of Submission:
☐ Preapplication
☐ Application
☐ Changed/Corrected Application

* 2. Type of Application:
☐ New
☐ Continuation
☐ Revision

* If Revision, select appropriate letter(s):

* Other (Specify)

* 3. Date Received:
Completed by Grants.gov upon submission.

4. Applicant Identifier:

5a. Federal Entity Identifier:

* 5b. Federal Award Identifier:

State Use Only:

6. Date Received by State:

7. State Application Identifier:

8. APPLICANT INFORMATION:

* a. Legal Name:

* b. Employer/Taxpayer Identification Number (EIN/TIN):

* c. Organizational DUNS:

d. Address:

* Street1:
Street2:
* City:
County:
* State:
Province:
* Country:
* Zip / Postal Code:

e. Organizational Unit:

Department Name:

Division Name:

f. Name and contact information of person to be contacted on matters involving this application:

Prefix:
Middle Name:
* Last Name:
Suffix:

* First Name:

Title:

Organizational Affiliation:

* Telephone Number:

Fax Number:

* Email:

FIG. 8-I (continued)

OMB Number: 4040-0004

Application for Federal Assistance SF-424	Version 02

9. Type of Applicant 1: Select Applicant Type:

Type of Applicant 2: Select Applicant Type:

Type of Applicant 3: Select Applicant Type:

* Other (specify):

* 10. Name of Federal Agency:

11. Catalog of Federal Domestic Assistance Number:

CFDA Title:

* 12. Funding Opportunity Number:

* Title:

13. Competition Identification Number:

Title:

14. Areas Affected by Project (Cities, Counties, States, etc.):

* 15. Descriptive Title of Applicant's Project:

Attach supporting documents as specified in agency instructions.

| Add Attachments | Delete Attachments | View Attachments |

©Thompson Publishing Group

FIG. 8-I (continued)

OMB Number: 4040-0004

Application for Federal Assistance SF-424	Version 02

16. Congressional Districts Of:

* a. Applicant [ ]   * b. Program/Project [ ]

Attach an additional list of Program/Project Congressional Districts if needed.

[ ] Add Attachment Delete Attachment View Attachment

17. Proposed Project:

* a. Start Date: [ ]   * b. End Date: [ ]

18. Estimated Funding ($):

* a. Federal [ ]

* b. Applicant [ ]

* c. State [ ]

* d. Local [ ]

* e. Other [ ]

* f. Program Income [ ]

* g. TOTAL [ ]

* 19. Is Application Subject to Review By State Under Executive Order 12372 Process?

☐ a. This application was made available to the State under the Executive Order 12372 Process for review on [ ] .

☐ b. Program is subject to E.O. 12372 but has not been selected by the State for review.

☐ c. Program is not covered by E.O. 12372.

* 20. Is the Applicant Delinquent On Any Federal Debt? (If "Yes", provide explanation.)

☐ Yes   ☐ No   Explanation

21. *By signing this application, I certify (1) to the statements contained in the list of certifications** and (2) that the statements herein are true, complete and accurate to the best of my knowledge. I also provide the required assurances** and agree to comply with any resulting terms if I accept an award. I am aware that any false, fictitious, or fraudulent statements or claims may subject me to criminal, civil, or administrative penalties. (U.S. Code, Title 218, Section 1001)*

☐ ** I AGREE

** The list of certifications and assurances, or an internet site where you may obtain this list, is contained in the announcement or agency specific instructions.

Authorized Representative:

Prefix: [ ]   * First Name: [ ]

Middle Name: [ ]

* Last Name: [ ]

Suffix: [ ]

* Title: [ ]

* Telephone Number: [ ]   Fax Number: [ ]

* Email: [ ]

* Signature of Authorized Representative: * Date Signed:

Authorized for Local Reproduction

Standard Form 424 (Revised 10/2005)
Prescribed by OMB Circular A-102

FIG. 8-I (continued)

OMB Number: 4040-0004

Application for Federal Assistance SF-424	Version 02

* Applicant Federal Debt Delinquency Explanation

The following field should contain an explanation if the Applicant organization is delinquent on any Federal Debt. Maximum number of characters that can be entered is 4,000. Try and avoid extra spaces and carriage returns to maximize the availability of space.

©Thompson Publishing Group

FIG. 8-1 (continued)

INSTRUCTIONS FOR THE SF-424

Public reporting burden for this collection of information is estimated to average 60 minutes per response, including time for reviewing instructions, searching existing data sources, gathering and maintaining the data needed, and completing and reviewing the collection of information. Send comments regarding the burden estimate or any other aspect of this collection of information, including suggestions for reducing this burden, to the Office of Management and Budget, Paperwork Reduction Project (0348-0043), Washington, DC 20503.

PLEASE DO NOT RETURN YOUR COMPLETED FORM TO THE OFFICE OF MANAGEMENT AND BUDGET. SEND IT TO THE ADDRESS PROVIDED BY THE SPONSORING AGENCY.

This is a standard form (including the continuation sheet) required for use as a cover sheet for submission of preapplications and applications and related information under discretionary programs. Some of the items are required and some are optional at the discretion of the applicant or the Federal agency (agency). Required items are identified with an asterisk on the form and are specified in the instructions below. In addition to the instructions provided below, applicants must consult agency instructions to determine specific requirements.

Item	Entry:	Item	Entry:
1.	**Type of Submission:** (Required): Select one type of submission in accordance with agency instructions. • Preapplication • Application • Changed/Corrected Application – If requested by the agency, check if this submission is to change or correct a previously submitted application. Unless requested by the agency, applicants may not use this to submit changes after the closing date.	10.	**Name Of Federal Agency:** (Required) Enter the name of the Federal agency from which assistance is being requested with this application.
		11.	**Catalog Of Federal Domestic Assistance Number/Title:** Enter the Catalog of Federal Domestic Assistance number and title of the program under which assistance is requested, as found in the program announcement, if applicable.
2.	**Type of Application:** (Required) Select one type of application in accordance with agency instructions. • New – An application that is being submitted to an agency for the first time. • Continuation - An extension for an additional funding/budget period for a project with a projected completion date. This can include renewals. • Revision - Any change in the Federal Government's financial obligation or contingent liability from an existing obligation. If a revision, enter the appropriate letter(s). More than one may be selected. If "Other" is selected, please specify in text box provided. A. Increase Award B. Decrease Award C. Increase Duration D. Decrease Duration E. Other (specify)	12.	**Funding Opportunity Number/Title:** (Required) Enter the Funding Opportunity Number and title of the opportunity under which assistance is requested, as found in the program announcement.
		13.	**Competition Identification Number/Title:** Enter the Competition Identification Number and title of the competition under which assistance is requested, if applicable.
		14.	**Areas Affected By Project:** List the areas or entities using the categories (e.g., cities, counties, states, etc.) specified in agency instructions. Use the continuation sheet to enter additional areas, if needed.
3.	**Date Received:** Leave this field blank. This date will be assigned by the Federal agency.	15.	**Descriptive Title of Applicant's Project:** (Required) Enter a brief descriptive title of the project. If appropriate, attach a map showing project location (e.g., construction or real property projects). For preapplications, attach a summary description of the project.
4.	**Applicant Identifier:** Enter the entity identifier assigned by the Federal agency, if any, or applicant's control number, if applicable.		
5a	**Federal Entity Identifier:** Enter the number assigned to your organization by the Federal Agency, if any.	16.	**Congressional Districts Of:** (Required) 16a. Enter the applicant's Congressional District, and 16b. Enter all District(s) affected by the program or project. Enter in the format: 2 characters State Abbreviation – 3 characters District Number, e.g., CA-005 for California 5th district, CA-012 for California 12th district, NC-103 for North Carolina's 103rd district. • If all congressional districts in a state are affected, enter "all" for the district number, e.g., MD-all for all congressional districts in Maryland. • If nationwide, i.e. all districts within all states are affected, enter US-all. • If the program/project is outside the US, enter 00-000.
5b.	**Federal Award Identifier:** For new applications leave blank. For a continuation or revision to an existing award, enter the previously assigned Federal award identifier number. If a changed/corrected application, enter the Federal Identifier in accordance with agency instructions.		
6.	**Date Received by State:** Leave this field blank. This date will be assigned by the State, if applicable.		
7.	**State Application Identifier:** Leave this field blank. This identifier will be assigned by the State, if applicable.		
8.	**Applicant Information:** Enter the following in accordance with agency instructions:	17.	**Proposed Project Start and End Dates:** (Required) Enter the proposed start date and end date of the project.
	a. Legal Name: (Required): Enter the legal name of applicant that will undertake the assistance activity. This is the name that the organization has registered with the Central Contractor Registry. Information on registering with CCR may be obtained by visiting the Grants.gov website.		
	b. Employer/Taxpayer Number (EIN/TIN): (Required): Enter the Employer or Taxpayer Identification Number (EIN or TIN) as assigned by the Internal Revenue Service. If your organization is not in the US, enter 44-4444444.	18.	**Estimated Funding:** (Required) Enter the amount requested or to be contributed during the first funding/budget period by each contributor. Value of in-kind contributions should be included on appropriate lines, as applicable. If the action will result in a dollar change to an existing award, indicate only the amount of the change. For decreases, enclose the amounts in parentheses.
	c. Organizational DUNS: (Required) Enter the organization's DUNS or DUNS+4 number received from Dun and Bradstreet. Information on obtaining a DUNS number may be obtained by visiting the Grants.gov website.		
	d. Address: Enter the complete address as follows: Street address (Line 1 required), City (Required), County, State (Required, if country is US), Province, Country (Required), Zip/Postal Code (Required, if country is US).	19.	**Is Application Subject to Review by State Under Executive Order 12372 Process?** Applicants should contact the State Single Point of Contact (SPOC) for Federal Executive Order 12372 to determine whether the application is subject to the
	e. Organizational Unit: Enter the name of the primary organizational unit (and department or division, if applicable) that will undertake the		

FIG. 8-I (continued)

	assistance activity, if applicable.		State intergovernmental review process. Select the appropriate box. If "a." is selected, enter the date the application was submitted to the State
	f. Name and contact information of person to be contacted on matters involving this application: Enter the name (First and last name required), organizational affiliation (if affiliated with an organization other than the applicant organization), telephone number (Required), fax number, and email address (Required) of the person to contact on matters related to this application.	20.	**Is the Applicant Delinquent on any Federal Debt?** (Required) Select the appropriate box. This question applies to the applicant organization, not the person who signs as the authorized representative. Categories of debt include delinquent audit disallowances, loans and taxes. If yes, include an explanation on the continuation sheet.
9.	Type of Applicant: (Required) Select up to three applicant type(s) in accordance with agency instructions.	21.	**Authorized Representative**: (Required) To be signed and dated by the authorized representative of the applicant organization. Enter the name (First and last name required) title (Required), telephone number (Required), fax number, and email address (Required) of the person authorized to sign for the applicant. A copy of the governing body's authorization for you to sign this application as the official representative must be on file in the applicant's office. (Certain Federal agencies may require that this authorization be submitted as part of the application.)

Type of Applicant list (item 9):

A. State Government
B. County Government
C. City or Township Government
D. Special District Government
E. Regional Organization
F. U.S. Territory or Possession
G. Independent School District
H. Public/State Controlled Institution of Higher Education
I. Indian/Native American Tribal Government (Federally Recognized)
J. Indian/Native American Tribal Government (Other than Federally Recognized)
K. Indian/Native American Tribally Designated Organization
L. Public/Indian Housing Authority

M. Nonprofit with 501C3 IRS Status (Other than Institution of Higher Education)
N. Nonprofit without 501C3 IRS Status (Other than Institution of Higher Education)
O. Private Institution of Higher Education
P. Individual
Q. For-Profit Organization (Other than Small Business)
R. Small Business
S. Hispanic-serving Institution
T. Historically Black Colleges and Universities (HBCUs)
U. Tribally Controlled Colleges and Universities (TCCUs)
V. Alaska Native and Native Hawaiian Serving Institutions
W. Non-domestic (non-US) Entity
X. Other (specify)

©Thompson Publishing Group

SF-424A

Standard Form 424A (see Fig. 8-2) is the budget information form for grant applications requesting funds for non-construction projects.

Fig. 8-2

BUDGET INFORMATION - Non-Construction Programs

OMB Approval No. 0348-0044

SECTION A - BUDGET SUMMARY

Grant Program Function or Activity (a)	Catalog of Federal Domestic Assistance Number (b)	Estimated Unobligated Funds		New or Revised Budget		
		Federal (c)	Non-Federal (d)	Federal (e)	Non-Federal (f)	Total (g)
1.		$	$	$	$	$
2.						
3.						
4.						
5. Totals		$	$	$	$	$

SECTION B - BUDGET CATEGORIES

6. Object Class Categories	GRANT PROGRAM, FUNCTION OR ACTIVITY				Total
	(1)	(2)	(3)	(4)	(5)
a. Personnel	$	$	$	$	$
b. Fringe Benefits					
c. Travel					
d. Equipment					
e. Supplies					
f. Contractual					
g. Construction					
h. Other					
i. Total Direct Charges (sum of 6a-6h)					$
j. Indirect Charges					$
k. TOTALS (sum of 6i and 6j)	$	$	$	$	$
7. Program Income	$	$	$	$	$

Authorized for Local Reproduction

Standard Form 424A (Rev. 7- 97)
Prescribed by OMB (Circular A -102)

FIG. 8-2 (continued)

SECTION C - NON-FEDERAL RESOURCES

(a) Grant Program	(b) Applicant	(c) State	(d) Other Sources	(e) TOTALS
8.	$	$	$	$
9.				
10.				
11.				
12. TOTAL (sum of lines 8-11)	$	$	$	$

SECTION D - FORECASTED CASH NEEDS

	Total for 1st Year	1st Quarter	2nd Quarter	3rd Quarter	4th Quarter
13. Federal	$	$	$	$	$
14. Non-Federal	$				
15. TOTAL (sum of lines 13 and 14)	$	$	$	$	$

SECTION E - BUDGET ESTIMATES OF FEDERAL FUNDS NEEDED FOR BALANCE OF THE PROJECT

(a) Grant Program	FUTURE FUNDING PERIODS (Years)			
	(b) First	(c) Second	(d) Third	(e) Fourth
16.	$	$	$	$
17.				
18.				
19.				
20. TOTAL (sum of lines 16 - 19)	$	$	$	$

SECTION F - OTHER BUDGET INFORMATION

21. Direct Charges:	22. Indirect Charges:

23. Remarks:

Authorized for Local Reproduction

Standard Form 424A (Rev. 7-97) Page 2

©Thompson Publishing Group

SF-424C

Standard Form 424C (Fig. 8-3) is the budget information form for grant applications requesting funds for construction projects.

Fig. 8-3

BUDGET INFORMATION - Construction Programs

OMB Approval No. 0348-0041

NOTE: Certain Federal assistance programs require additional computations to arrive at the Federal share of project costs eligible for participation. If such is the case, you will be notified.

COST CLASSIFICATION	a. Total Cost	b. Costs Not Allowable for Participation	c. Total Allowable Costs (Columns a-b)
1. Administrative and legal expenses	$	$	$
2. Land, structures, rights-of-way, appraisals, etc.	$	$	$
3. Relocation expenses and payments	$	$	$
4. Architectual and engineering fees	$	$	$
5. Other architectural and engineering fees	$	$	$
6. Project inspection fees	$	$	$
7. Site work	$	$	$
8. Demolition and removal	$	$	$
9. Construction	$	$	$
10. Equipment	$	$	$
11. Miscellaneous	$	$	$
12. SUBTOTAL *(sum of lines 1-11)*	$	$	$
13. Contingencies	$	$	$
14. SUBTOTAL	$	$	$
15. Project (program) income	$	$	$
16. TOTAL PROJECT COSTS *(subtract #15 from #14)*	$	$	$

FEDERAL FUNDING

17. Federal assistance requested, calculate as follows: (Consult Federal agency for Federal percentage share.) Enter the resulting Federal share.	Enter eligible costs from line 16c Multiply X ____ %	$

Previous Edition Usable **Authorized for Local Reproduction** **Standard Form 424C (Rev. 7-97) Prescribed by OMB Circular A-102**

SF-424 Research and Related Forms

Standard Form 424 R&R (Fig. 8-4) was first used in November 2004 by federal agencies with a research mission or agencies that conduct research-related activities.

There are several other forms required for grant applications proposing research. Here's a list of these research and related forms:

*   Budget

*   Project/Performance Site Locations(s)

*   Senior/Key Person Profile

*   Personal Data

*   Other Project Information

*   Subaward Budget Attachment(s) Form

*   Senior/Key Person Profile (Expanded)

*   Budget (Total federal and nonfederal funds)

*   Subaward Budget (Total federal and nonfederal funds) Attachment(s) Form

*   Attachments Form

See page 129 for the Web link for these related forms.

©Thompson Publishing Group

FIG. 8-4

| APPLICATION FOR FEDERAL ASSISTANCE **SF 424 (R&R)** | 2. DATE SUBMITTED | Applicant Identifier |
| | 3. DATE RECEIVED BY STATE | State Application Identifier |

1. * TYPE OF SUBMISSION

☐ Pre-application ☐ Application
☐ Changed/Corrected Application

4. Federal Identifier

5. APPLICANT INFORMATION   * Organizational DUNS:

* Legal Name:

Department: Division:

* Street1:   Street2:

* City: County: * State: * ZIP Code:

* Country:

Person to be contacted on matters involving this application

Prefix: * First Name: Middle Name: * Last Name: Suffix:

* Phone Number: Fax Number: Email:

6. * EMPLOYER IDENTIFICATION *(EIN) or (TIN):*

7. * TYPE OF APPLICANT:

Please select one of the following

8. * TYPE OF APPLICATION: ☐ New

☐ Resubmission ☐ Renewal ☐ Continuation ☐ Revision

Other (Specify):

Small Business Organization Type

▣ Women Owned   ▣ Socially and Economically Disadvantaged

If Revision, mark appropriate box(es).

▣ A. Increase Award ▣ B. Decrease Award ▣ C. Increase Duration

▣ D. Decrease Duration ▣ E. Other *(specify)*

* Is this application being submitted to other agencies?   Yes☐ No☐

What other Agencies?

9. * NAME OF FEDERAL AGENCY:

10. CATALOG OF FEDERAL DOMESTIC ASSISTANCE NUMBER:

TITLE:

11. * DESCRIPTIVE TITLE OF APPLICANT'S PROJECT:

12. * AREAS AFFECTED BY PROJECT *(cities, counties, states, etc.)*

13. PROPOSED PROJECT:

* Start Date   * Ending Date

14. CONGRESSIONAL DISTRICTS OF:

a. * Applicant   b. * Project

15. PROJECT DIRECTOR/PRINCIPAL INVESTIGATOR CONTACT INFORMATION

Prefix: * First Name: Middle Name: * Last Name: Suffix:

Position/Title: * Organization Name:

Department: Division:

* Street1:   Street2:

* City: County: * State: * ZIP Code:

* Country:

* Phone Number: Fax Number: * Email:

OMB Number: 4040-0001
Expiration Date: 04/30/2008

FIG. 8-4 (continued)

SF 424 (R&R) APPLICATION FOR FEDERAL ASSISTANCE — Page 2

16. ESTIMATED PROJECT FUNDING

a. * Total Estimated Project Funding

b. * Total Federal & Non-Federal Funds

c. * Estimated Program Income

17. * IS APPLICATION SUBJECT TO REVIEW BY STATE EXECUTIVE ORDER 12372 PROCESS?

a. YES ☐ THIS PREAPPLICATION/APPLICATION WAS MADE AVAILABLE TO THE STATE EXECUTIVE ORDER 12372 PROCESS FOR REVIEW ON:

DATE:

b. NO ☐ PROGRAM IS NOT COVERED BY E.O. 12372; OR

☐ PROGRAM HAS NOT BEEN SELECTED BY STATE FOR REVIEW

18. By signing this application, I certify (1) to the statements contained in the list of certifications* and (2) that the statements herein are true, complete and accurate to the best of my knowledge. I also provide the required assurances * and agree to comply with any resulting terms if I accept an award. I am aware that any false, fictitious, or fraudulent statements or claims may subject me to criminal, civil, or administrative penalties. (U.S. Code, Title 18, Section 1001)

☐ * I agree

* The list of certifications and assurances, or an Internet site where you may obtain this list, is contained in the announcement or agency specific instructions.

19. Authorized Representative

Prefix: | * First Name: | Middle Name: | * Last Name: | Suffix:

* Position/Title: | * Organization:

Department: | Division:

* Street1: | Street2:

* City: | County: | * State: | * ZIP Code:

* Country:

* Phone Number: | Fax Number: | * Email:

* Signature of Authorized Representative | * Date Signed

20. Pre-application [Add Attachment] [Delete Attachment] [View Attachment]

21. Attach an additional list of Project Congressional Districts if needed.
[Add Attachment] [Delete Attachment] [View Attachment]

OMB Number: 4040-0001
Expiration Date: 04/30/2008

©Thompson Publishing Group

SF-424 Mandatory (M)

Standard Form 424-Mandatory (Fig. 8-5) was first used in February 2005 by federal agencies with mandatory grant programs, including formula and block grants. See page 129 for the Web link for the SF-424 M form and instructions.

FIG. 8-5

APPLICATION FOR FEDERAL ASSISTANCE SF-424 - MANDATORY	Version 01.1

* 1.a. Type of Submission:
- ☐ Application
- ☐ Plan
- ☐ Funding Request
- ☐ Other

* Other (specify)

* 1.b. Frequency:
- ☐ Annual
- ☐ Quarterly
- ☐ Other

* Other (specify)

* 1.d. Version:
☐ Initial   ☐ Resubmission   ☐ Revision   ☐ Update

* 2. Date Received: **STATE USE ONLY:**

3. Applicant Identifier: **5. Date Received by State:**

4a. Federal Entity Identifier: **6. State Application Identifier:**

4b. Federal Award Identifier:

1.c. Consolidated Application/Plan/Funding Request?
Yes ☐   No ☐   [Explanation]

7. APPLICANT INFORMATION:

* a. Legal Name:

* b. Employer/Taxpayer Identification Number (EIN/TIN):   *** c. Organizational DUNS:**

d. Address:

* Street1:   **Street2:**

* City: **County:**

* State: **Province:**

* Country: *** Zip / Postal Code:**

e. Organizational Unit:

Department Name: Division Name:

f. Name and contact information of person to be contacted on matters involving this submission:

Prefix: * First Name: Middle Name:

* Last Name: Suffix:

Title:

Organizational Affiliation:

* Telephone Number: Fax Number:

* Email:

Authorized for Local Reproduction

Standard Form 424 Mandatory (Effective 08/2005)
Prescribed by OMB Circular A-102

FIG. 8-5 (continued)

OMB Number: 4040-0002
Expiration Date: 08/31/2008

APPLICATION FOR FEDERAL ASSISTANCE SF-424 - MANDATORY   Version 01.1

* 8a. TYPE OF APPLICANT:

* Other (specify):

b. Additional Description:

* 9. Name of Federal Agency:

10. Catalog of Federal Domestic Assistance Number:

CFDA Title:

11. Areas Affected by Funding:

12. CONGRESSIONAL DISTRICTS OF:

* a. Applicant: b. Program/Project:

Attach an additional list of Program/Project Congressional Districts if needed.

Add Attachment   Delete Attachment   View Attachment

13. FUNDING PERIOD:

a. Start Date: b. End Date:

14. ESTIMATED FUNDING:

* a. Federal ($):   b. Match ($):

* 15. IS SUBMISSION SUBJECT TO REVIEW BY STATE UNDER EXECUTIVE ORDER 12372 PROCESS?

☐ a. This submission was made available to the State under the Executive Order 12372 Process for review on:

☐ b. Program is subject to E.O. 12372 but has not been selected by State for review.

☐ c. Program is not covered by E.O. 12372.

Authorized for Local Reproduction

Standard Form 424 Mandatory (Effective 08/2005)
Prescribed by OMB Circular A-102

©Thompson Publishing Group

FIG. 8-5 (continued)

OMB Number: 4040-0002
Expiration Date: 08/31/2008

APPLICATION FOR FEDERAL ASSISTANCE SF-424 - MANDATORY	Version 01.1

* 16. Is The Applicant Delinquent On Any Federal Debt?

Yes ☐   No ☐   Explanation

17. By signing this application, I certify (1) to the statements contained in the list of certifications** and (2) that the statements herein are true, complete and accurate to the best of my knowledge. I also provide the required assurances** and agree to comply with any resulting terms if I accept an award. I am aware that any false, fictitious, or fraudulent statements or claims may subject me to criminal, civil, or administrative penalties. (U.S. Code, Title 218, Section 1001)

** I Agree ☐

** This list of certifications and assurances, or an internet site where you may obtain this list, is contained in the announcement or agency specific instructions.

Authorized Representative:

Prefix:

* First Name:

Middle Name:

* Last Name:

Suffix:

* Title:

Organizational Affiliation:

* Telephone Number:

* Fax Number:

* Email:

* Signature of Authorized Representative:

* Date Signed:

Attach supporting documents as specified in agency instructions.

Add Attachments Delete Attachments View Attachments

Authorized for Local Reproduction

Standard Form 424 Mandatory (Effective 08/2005)
Prescribed by OMB Circular A-102

FIG. 8-5 (continued)

OMB Number: 4040-0002
Expiration Date: 08/31/2008

APPLICATION FOR FEDERAL ASSISTANCE SF-424 - MANDATORY	Version 01.1

* Consolidated Application/Plan/Funding Request Explanation:

Authorized for Local Reproduction

Standard Form 424 Mandatory (Effective 08/2005)
Prescribed by OMB Circular A-102

©Thompson Publishing Group

FIG. 8-5 (continued)

OMB Number: 4040-0002
Expiration Date: 08/31/2008

APPLICATION FOR FEDERAL ASSISTANCE SF-424 - MANDATORY	Version 01.1

* Applicant Federal Debt Delinquency Explanation:

Authorized for Local Reproduction

Standard Form 424 Mandatory (Effective 08/2005)
Prescribed by OMB Circular A-102

SF-424 Short Organizational Form

Standard Form 424-Short Organizational (Fig. 8-6) was first used in June 2005 to provide agencies a streamlined form for grant programs that do not have to collect certain applicant information that is a standard part of the SF-424 core data set and form.

FIG. 8-6

OMB Number: 4040-0003
Expiration Date: 01/31/2007

APPLICATION FOR FEDERAL DOMESTIC ASSISTANCE - Short Organizational

Version 01

* 1. NAME OF FEDERAL AGENCY:

2. CATALOG OF FEDERAL DOMESTIC ASSISTANCE NUMBER:

CFDA TITLE:

* 3. DATE RECEIVED: SYSTEM USE ONLY

* 4. FUNDING OPPORTUNITY NUMBER:

* TITLE:

5. APPLICANT INFORMATION

* a. Legal Name:

b. Address:

* Street1:   Street2:

* City: County:

* State: Province:

* Country: * Zip/Postal Code:

c. Web Address:
http://

* d. Type of Applicant: Select Applicant Type Code(s):   * e. Employer/Taxpayer Identification Number (EIN/TIN):

Type of Applicant: * f. Organizational DUNS:

Type of Applicant: * g. Congressional District of Applicant:

* Other (specify):

6. PROJECT INFORMATION

* a. Project Title:

* b. Project Description:

c. Proposed Project: * Start Date: * End Date:

©Thompson Publishing Group

FIG. 8-6 (continued)

OMB Number: 4040-0003
Expiration Date: 01/31/2007

APPLICATION FOR FEDERAL DOMESTIC ASSISTANCE - Short Organizational	Version 01

7. PROJECT DIRECTOR

Social Security Number (SSN) - Optional:

Disclosure of SSN is voluntary. Please see the application package instructions for the agency's authority and routine uses of the data.

Prefix:	* First Name:	Middle Name:

* Last Name:	Suffix:

* Title:	* Email:

* Telephone Number:	Fax Number:

* Street1:	Street2:

* City:	County:

* State:	Province:

* Country:	* Zip/Postal Code:

8. PRIMARY CONTACT/GRANTS ADMINISTRATOR

☐ Same as Project Director (skip to item 9):

Social Security Number (SSN) - Optional:

Disclosure of SSN is voluntary. Please see the application package instructions for the agency's authority and routine uses of the data.

Prefix:	* First Name:	Middle Name:

* Last Name:	Suffix:

* Title:	* Email:

* Telephone Number:	Fax Number:

* Street1:	Street2:

* City:	County:

* State:	Province:

* Country:	* Zip/Postal Code:

FIG. 8-6 (continued)

OMB Number: 4040-0003
Expiration Date: 01/31/2007

APPLICATION FOR FEDERAL DOMESTIC ASSISTANCE - **Short Organizational**	Version 01

9. * By signing this application, I certify (1) to the statements contained in the list of certifications** and (2) that the statements herein are true, complete and accurate to the best of my knowledge. I also provide the required assurances** and agree to comply with any resulting terms if I accept an award. I am aware that any false, fictitious, or fraudulent statements or claims may subject me to criminal, civil, or administrative penalties (U.S. Code, Title 218, Section 1001)

** I Agree ☐

** The list of certifications and assurances, or an internet site where you may obtain this list, is contained in the announcement or agency specific instructions.

AUTHORIZED REPRESENTATIVE

Prefix:	* First Name:	Middle Name:

* Last Name:	Suffix:

* Title:	* Email:

* Telephone Number:	Fax Number:

* Signature of Authorized Representative:	* Date Signed:

Authorized for Local Reproduction

Standard Form 424 Organization Short (04-2005)
Prescribed by OMB Circular A-102

©Thompson Publishing Group

SF-424 Individual (I)

Standard Form 424-Individual (Fig. 8-7) provides agencies with streamlined data from applicants who are individuals rather than organizations. See page 129 for the Web link for the SF-424 I form and instructions.

FIG. 8-7

OMB Number: 4040-0005
Expiration Date: 01/31/2007

APPLICATION FOR FEDERAL ASSISTANCE SF 424 - INDIVIDUAL   Version 01

* 1. NAME OF FEDERAL AGENCY:

2. CATALOG OF FEDERAL DOMESTIC ASSISTANCE NUMBER: **CFDA TITLE:**

* 3. DATE RECEIVED:

* 4. FUNDING OPPORTUNITY NUMBER:

* TITLE:

5. APPLICANT INFORMATION

a. Name and Contact Information

Prefix: * First Name: Middle Name:

* Last Name: Suffix:

* Telephone Number (Daytime):   Telephone Number (Evening):

Email: Fax Number:

b. Address

* Street1:   Street2:

* City: County:

* State: Province:

* Country: * Zip/Postal Code:

FIG. 8-7 (continued)

OMB Number: 4040-0005
Expiration Date: 01/31/2007

| APPLICATION FOR FEDERAL ASSISTANCE SF 424 - INDIVIDUAL | Version 01 |

* c. Citizenship Status:

U.S. Citizenship   ☐ Yes   ☐ No

If No

If permanent resident of U.S., enter the Alien Registration #:

* If foreign national, enter country of citizenship:

* If foreign national, enter start date of most recent residency in U.S.:

d. Social Security Number (SSN) - Optional:

Disclosure of SSN is voluntary. Please see the application package instructions for the agency's authority and routine uses of the data.

e. * Congressional District of Applicant:

6. PROJECT INFORMATION

a. Project Title:

* b. Project Description:

* c. Proposed Project: Start Date: End Date:

7. * By signing this application, I certify (1) to the statements contained in the list of certifications** and (2) that the statements herein are true, complete and accurate to the best of my knowledge. I also provide the required assurances** and agree to comply with any resulting terms if I accept an award. I am aware that any false, fictitious, or fraudulent statements or claims may subject me to criminal, civil, or administrative penalties (U.S. Code, Title 218, Section 1001)

** I Agree ☐

** The list of certifications and assurances, or an internet site where you may obtain this list, is contained in the announcement or agency specific instructions.

* Signature: *** Date Signed:**

Authorized for Local Reproduction

Standard Form 424 Individual (05-2005)
Prescribed by OMB Circular A-102

©Thompson Publishing Group

SF-424 Supplemental Forms

The SF-424 Supplemental Key Contacts form helps agencies collect additional key contact or point of contact information. The SF-424 Supplemental Project Abstract helps agencies collect project abstract information.

Federal grant application forms are available at the Grants.gov site, http://www.grants.gov/agencies/approved_standard_forms.jsp#1

Private Grant Application Forms

Regional Associations of Grantmakers

The Forum of Regional Associations of Grantmakers is a national network of funding organizations that award grants of all types. Presently, there are 32 regional associations representing more than 4,000 funders. The forum's Web site can be found at: http://www.givingforum.org.

Common Grant Application Forms

This Web site is an important resource for grant writers who plan to approach foundation and corporate grantmakers in states with regional associations. Most regional associations have their own grant application forms and formats – commonly called Common Grant Applications. A sample Common Grant Application is printed on page 131.

Not all regional associations have common grant applications. Here's a list of the most current regional associations with state- or region-specific grant writing forms and formats:

- Associated Grant Makers (MA)
- Association of Baltimore Area Grantmakers
- Colorado Association of Funders
- Connecticut Council for Philanthropy
- Council of Michigan Foundations
- Council of New Jersey Grantmakers
- Delaware Valley Grantmakers
- Donors Forum of Chicago
- Donors Forum of Wisconsin
- Grantmakers Forum of New York
- Grantmakers of Western Pennsylvania

COMMON GRANT APPLICATION TIPS

I've filled out most of the common grant application forms available from the regional associations. The best way to expedite completing a common grant application is to download the templates (if not already in Microsoft Word format) and retype them in Word. If you create a working template for your region, you can simply open up the template each time you plan to apply for a regional association member grant and save as your current project's name. This way you'll only have to type headings, subheadings and bullets one time.

- Minnesota Council on Foundations

- New York Regional Association of Grantmakers

- Philanthropy Northwest

- Washington Grantmakers

If you go to the Giving Forum's home Web page, you'll be able to locate the link for the regional associations. You can click on the link (found in the list above online) to visit each regional association and download its application form(s), if available. One regional association that does not appear on this list is the one in Arizona. If you conduct a search on the Giving Forum's home Web page (type in Arizona), you'll find this information:

Arizona Grantmakers Forum

Arizona Grantmakers Forum
2201 E. Camelback Road, Suite 202
Phoenix, AZ 85016
Phone: (602) 977-2756
Fax: (602) 682-2059
Email: info@arizonagrantmakersforum.org
Web address: www.arizonagrantmakersforum.org

Arizona now has a common grant application form.

The Minnesota Common Grant Application Form which follows is reprinted with the permission of the Minnesota Council on Foundations (http://www.mcf.org; 612-338-1989).

©Thompson Publishing Group

Fig. 8-8

Minnesota Common Grant Application Form
Grant Application Cover Sheet
You may reproduce this form on your computer

Date of application: _____ Application submitted to: _____

Organization Information

_____
Name of organization | Legal name, if different

_____
Address | City, State, Zip | Employer Identification Number (EIN)

_____
Phone | Fax | Web site

_____
Name of top paid staff | Title | Phone | E-mail

_____
Name of contact person regarding this application | Title | Phone | E-mail

Is your organization an IRS 501(c)(3) not-for-profit? _____ Yes _____ No

If no, is your organization a public agency/unit of government? _____ Yes _____ No

If no, check with funder for details on using fiscal agents, and list name and address of fiscal agent:

_____
_____ Fiscal agent's EIN number

Proposal Information

Please give a 2-3 sentence summary of request:

Population served: Geographic area served:

Funds are being requested for (check one) *Note: Please be sure funder provides the type of support you are requesting.*

_____ General operating support _____ Start-up costs _____ Capital
_____ Project/program support _____ Technical assistance _____ Other (list) _____

Project dates (if applicable): _____ Fiscal year end: _____

Budget

Dollar amount requested: $ _____
Total annual organization budget: $ _____
Total project budget (for support other than general operating): $ _____

Authorization

Name and title of top paid staff or board chair: _____
Signature _____

12/2000

FIG. 8-8 (continued)

Minnesota Common Grant Application Form

PROPOSAL NARRATIVE

Please use the following outline as a guide to your proposal narrative. Most grantmakers prefer up to five pages, excluding attachments, but *be sure to ask each individual funder if they have page limitations or any additional requirements.* Also, include a cover letter with your application that introduces your organization and proposal and makes the link between your proposal and the mission of the grantmaker to whom you are applying. For assistance with terms, refer to MCF's Web site (www.mcf.org; select "Grantseeking in Minnesota").

I. ORGANIZATION INFORMATION

A. Brief summary of organization history, including the date your organization was established.
B. Brief summary of organization mission and goals.
C. Brief description of organization's current programs or activities, including any service statistics and strengths or accomplishments. Please highlight new or different activities, if any, for your organization.
D. Your organization's relationship with other organizations working with similar missions. What is your organization's role relative to these organizations?
E. Number of board members, full-time paid staff, part-time paid staff and volunteers.
F. Additional organization information required by each individual funder.

II. PURPOSE OF GRANT

General operating proposals: Complete Section A below and move to Part III - Evaluation.
All other proposal types: Complete Section B below and move to Part III - Evaluation.

A. General Operating Proposals
1. The opportunity, challenges, issues or need currently facing your organization.
2. Overall goal(s) of the organization for the funding period.
3. Objectives or ways in which you will meet the goal(s).
4. Activities and who will carry out these activities.
5. Time frame in which this will take place.
6. Long-term funding strategies.
7. Additional information regarding general operating proposals required by each individual funder.

B. All Other Proposal Types
1. Situation
   a. The opportunity, challenges, issues or need and the community that your proposal addresses.
   b. How that focus was determined and who was involved in that decision-making process.
2. Activities
   a. Overall goal(s) regarding the situation described above.
   b. Objectives or ways in which you will meet the goal(s).
   c. Specific activities for which you seek funding.
   d. Who will carry out those activities.
   e. Time frame in which this will take place.
   f. How the proposed activities will benefit the community in which they will occur, being as clear as you can about the impact you expect to have.
   g. Long-term funding strategies (if applicable) for sustaining this effort.

12/2000

©Thompson Publishing Group

FIG. 8-8 (continued)

Minnesota Common Grant Application Form

III. EVALUATION

A. Please describe your criteria for success. What do you want to happen as a result of your activities? You may find it helpful to describe both immediate and long-term effects.
B. How will you measure these changes?
C. Who will be involved in evaluating this work (staff, board, constituents, community, consultants)?
D. What will you do with your evaluation results?

ATTACHMENTS

Generally the following attachments are required:

1. Finances (*for assistance with terms, check MCF's Web site at www.mcf.org.*)
   - Most recent financial statement from most recently completed year, audited if available, showing actual expenses. This information should include a balance sheet, a statement of activities (or statement of income and expenses) and functional expenses. Some funders require your most recent Form 990 tax return.
   - Organization budget for current year, including income and expenses.
   - Project Budget, including income and expenses (if not a general operating proposal).
   - Additional funders. List names of corporations and foundations from which you are requesting funds, with dollar amounts, indicating which sources are committed or pending.

2. List of board members and their affiliations.
3. Brief description of key staff, including qualifications relevant to the specific request.
4. A copy of your current IRS determination letter (or your fiscal agent's) indicating tax-exempt 501(c)(3) status.
5. If applying to a corporate funder only: if an employee of this corporation is involved with your organization, list names and involvement.

Be sure to check each funder's guidelines, and use discretion when sending additional attachments.

PROPOSAL CHECKLIST

- ❑ Cover letter.
- ❑ Cover sheet.
- ❑ Proposal narrative.
- ❑ Organization budget.
- ❑ Project budget (if not general operating grant).
- ❑ Financial statements, preferably audited, showing actual expenses including:
  - ❑ Balance sheet.
  - ❑ Statement of activities (income and expenses).
  - ❑ Statement of functional expenses.
- ❑ List of additional funders.

- ❑ List of board members and their affiliations.
- ❑ Brief description of key staff.
- ❑ IRS determination letter.
- ❑ Confirmation letter of fiscal agent (if required).
- ❑ Additional information required by each individual funder.

12/2000

Minnesota Common Grant Application Form

ORGANIZATION BUDGET

This format is optional and can serve as a guide to budgeting. If you already prepare an organization budget that contains this information, please feel free to submit it in its original form. Feel free to attach a budget narrative explaining your numbers if necessary.

INCOME

Source	Amount
Support	
Government grants	$
Foundations	$
Corporations	$
United Way or other federated campaigns	$
Individual contributions	$
Fundraising events and products	$
Membership income	$
In-kind support	$
Investment income	$
Revenue	
Government contracts	$
Earned income	$
Other (specify)	$
	$
	$
	$
Total Income	**$**

EXPENSES

Item	Amount
Salaries and wages	$
Insurance, benefits and other related taxes	$
Consultants and professional fees	$
Travel	$
Equipment	$
Supplies	$
Printing and copying	$
Telephone and fax	$
Postage and delivery	$
Rent and utilities	$
In-kind expenses	$
Depreciation	$
Other (specify)	$
	$
	$
Total Expense	**$**
Difference (Income less Expense)	**$**

12/2000

©Thompson Publishing Group

FIG. 8-8 (continued)

Minnesota Common Grant Application Form

PROJECT BUDGET

This format is optional and can serve as a guide to budgeting. If you already prepare project budgets that contain this information, please feel free to submit them in their original forms. Feel free to attach a budget narrative explaining your numbers if necessary.

INCOME

Source	Amount
Support	
Government grants	$
Foundations	$
Corporations	$
United Way or other federated campaigns	$
Individual contributions	$
Fundraising events and products	$
Membership income	$
In-kind support	$
Investment income	$
Revenue	
Government contracts	$
Earned income	$
Other (specify)	$
	$
Total Income	**$**

EXPENSES

Item	Amount	%FT/PT
Salaries and wages (breakdown by individual position and indicate full- or part-time.)	$	
	$	
	$	
	$	
	$	
SUBTOTAL	$	
Insurance, benefits and other related taxes	$	
Consultants and professional fees	$	
Travel	$	
Equipment	$	
Supplies	$	
Printing and copying	$	
Telephone and fax	$	
Postage and delivery	$	
Rent and utilities	$	
In-kind expenses	$	
Depreciation	$	
Other (specify)	$	
	$	
Total Expense	**$**	
Difference (Income less Expense)	**$**	

12/2000

Resources for Grantseekers 9

In this final chapter, we'll take a look at a number of resources that are available to grantseekers to make their search for funding a little easier. Along with a series of listings from the Foundation Center ranking the top grantmaking foundations in the United States, also included is information on a number of Web sites that provide current information on available funding opportunities, as well as those that will connect you with a host of funding sources.

Also included in this chapter are the Web addresses for 26 federal grantmaking agencies. Although their funding opportunities will be listed on Grants.gov, you can always go to an individual agency's Web site to get the latest information on funding programs, as well as grantseeking assistance.

Remember, however, over time some of these Web site addresses may change slightly, so if you can't find a specific link listed, use a search engine to locate the most up-to-date Web address.

Largest U.S. Grantmaking Foundations

The following three tables highlight the top foundations in the United States based on a ranking from the Foundation Center. These tables are reprinted with the permission of the Foundation Center (www.fdncenter.org).

Top 100 U.S. Foundations by Total Giving

The following list is of the 100 largest U. S. grantmaking foundations ranked by total giving, based on the most current audited financial data in the Foundation Center's database as of July 27, 2006. Total giving figures include grants, scholarships, employee matching gifts and other amounts reported as "grants and contributions paid during the year" on the Internal Revenue Service 990-PF tax form. Total giving does not include all qualifying distributions under the tax law, e.g., loans, program-related investments, and program or other administrative expenses.

Rank	Name/(State)	Total Giving	As of Fiscal Year End Date
1.	Bill & Melinda Gates Foundation (WA) http://www.gatesfoundation.org/default.htm	$1,356,327,000	12/31/05
2.	Merck Patient Assistance Program, Inc. (NJ) http://www.merckhelps.com/patientassistance/	519,998,639	12/31/04
3.	The Ford Foundation (NY) http://www.fordfound.org/	511,679,000	09/30/05
4.	The Bristol-Myers Squibb Patient Assistance Foundation, Inc. (NJ) http://www.bms.com/sr/philanthropy/data/produc_patpr.html	506,639,972	12/31/04
5.	Lilly Endowment Inc. (IN) http://www.lillyendowment.org/	427,465,199	12/31/05
6.	The Robert Wood Johnson Foundation (NJ) http://www.rwjf.org/	359,500,275	12/31/04
7.	The William and Flora Hewlett Foundation (CA) http://www.hewlett.org/Default.htm	319,916,093	12/31/05
8.	Janssen Ortho Patient Assistance Foundation, Inc. (NJ)	289,783,393	12/31/04
9.	The Annenberg Foundation (PA) http://www.annenbergfoundation.org/	251,663,628	06/30/05
10.	Gordon and Betty Moore Foundation (CA) http://www.moore.org/	225,986,140	12/31/04
11.	W. K. Kellogg Foundation (MI) http://www.wkkf.org/Default.aspx?LanguageID=0	219,862,847	08/31/05
12.	John D. and Catherine T. MacArthur Foundation (IL) http://www.macfound.org/site/c.lkLXJ8MQKrH/b.855229/k.CC2B/Home.htm	209,996,176	12/31/04
13.	The Andrew W. Mellon Foundation (NY) http://www.mellon.org/	181,186,431	12/31/04
14.	The Roche Patient Assistance Foundation (NJ) http://www.rocheusa.com/programs/patientassist.asp	174,463,465	12/31/05
15.	The Annie E. Casey Foundation (MD) http://www.aecf.org/	171,354,926	12/31/04
16.	The Starr Foundation (NY) http://www.starrfoundation.org/	168,167,773	12/31/04
17.	Wal-Mart Foundation (AR) http://www.walmartfoundation.org/wmstore/good-works/scripts/index.jsp	154,537,406	01/31/05

©Thompson Publishing Group

Rank	Name/(State)	Total Giving	As of Fiscal Year End Date
18.	The California Endowment (CA) http://www.calendow.org/	153,242,789	02/28/05
19.	The David and Lucile Packard Foundation (CA) http://www.packard.org/home.aspx	150,115,645	12/31/05
20.	Boehringer Ingelheim Cares Foundation, Inc. (CT) http://us.boehringer-ingelheim.com/about/ philanthropy/philanthropy.html	147,996,554	12/31/05
21.	Lilly Cares Foundation, Inc. (IN) https://www.lillycares.com/index.jsp	146,701,709	12/31/04
22.	The Rockefeller Foundation (NY) http://www.rockfound.org/	143,202,709	12/31/04
23.	The New York Community Trust (NY) http://www.nycommunitytrust.org/	136,970,963	12/31/05
24.	Aventis Pharmaceuticals Health Care Foundation (NJ)	114,668,984	12/31/04
25.	Charles Stewart Mott Foundation (MI) http://www.mott.org/	113,334,381	12/31/05
26.	Peninsula Community Foundation (CA) http://www.pcf.org/	110,910,875	12/31/04
27.	The Duke Endowment (NC) http://www.dukeendowment.com/	105,774,927	12/31/04
28.	Walton Family Foundation, Inc. (AR) http://www.wffhome.com/	101,240,263	12/31/04
29.	Robert W. Woodruff Foundation, Inc. (GA) http://www.woodruff.org/	101,030,268	12/31/05
30.	The Harry and Jeanette Weinberg Foundation, Inc. (MD) http://www.hjweinbergfoundation.org/	98,674,477	02/28/05
31.	The Kresge Foundation (MI) http://www.kresge.org/	97,714,540	12/31/04
32.	John S. and James L. Knight Foundation (FL) http://www.knightfdn.org/	92,577,162	12/31/05
33.	The Ave Maria Foundation (MI) http://www.avemariafoundation.org/	91,925,690	12/31/04
34.	California Community Foundation (CA) http://www.calfund.org/	91,295,121	06/30/05
35.	Carnegie Corporation of New York (NY) http://www.carnegie.org/	91,053,489	09/30/05
36.	The McKnight Foundation (MN) http://www.mcknight.org/	90,710,176	12/31/05
37.	Open Society Institute (NY) http://www.soros.org/	83,470,616	12/31/04
38.	The Community Foundation for the National Capital Region (DC) http://www.cfncr.org/	83,251,153	03/31/05
39.	Foundation for the Carolinas (NC) http://www.fftc.org/	82,821,824	12/31/04
40.	The Bank of America Charitable Foundation, Inc. (NC) http://www.bankofamerica.com/foundation/index. cfm?template=fd_funding	80,734,705	12/31/04

Rank	Name/(State)	Total Giving	As of Fiscal Year End Date
41.	Ford Motor Company Fund (MI) http://www.ford.com/en/goodWorks/fundingAnd-Grants/fordMotorCompanyFund/default.htm	77,916,903	12/31/04
42.	The Chicago Community Trust (IL) http://www.cct.org/index.html	75,988,536	09/30/05
43.	Communities Foundation of Texas, Inc. (TX) http://www.cftexas.org/	75,853,025	06/30/05
44.	Community Foundation Silicon Valley (CA) http://www.cfsv.org/	75,366,593	06/30/05
45.	Richard King Mellon Foundation (PA) http://foundationcenter.org/grantmaker/rkmellon/	74,356,247	12/31/05
46.	Houston Endowment Inc. (TX) http://www.houstonendowment.org/	71,447,356	12/31/04
47.	Donald W. Reynolds Foundation (NV) http://www.dwreynolds.org/	69,203,364	12/31/05
48.	The Cleveland Foundation (OH) http://www.clevelandfoundation.org/	66,421,855	12/31/05
49.	The Wells Fargo Foundation (CA) https://www.wellsfargo.com/about/charitable/index.jhtml?_requestid=7003	64,747,007	12/31/04
50.	Boston Foundation, Inc. (MA) http://www.tbf.org/	64,092,145	06/30/05
51.	ExxonMobil Foundation (TX) http://www.exxonmobil.com/Corporate/Citizenship/gcr_mainpage_categories.asp	63,660,965	12/31/05
52.	Greater Kansas City Community Foundation (MO) http://www.gkccf.org/	63,388,075	12/31/04
53.	The San Francisco Foundation (CA) http://www.sff.org/	62,109,000	06/30/05
54.	Alfred P. Sloan Foundation (NY) http://www.sloan.org/	59,742,875	12/31/04
55.	The William Penn Foundation (PA) http://www.williampennfoundation.org/	59,476,104	12/31/04
56.	Doris Duke Charitable Foundation (NY) http://www.ddcf.org/	59,167,979	12/31/04
57.	The Robert W. Wilson Charitable Trust (NY)	58,759,248	12/31/04
58.	Citigroup Foundation (NY) http://www.citigroupfoundation.org/citigroup/corporate/foundation/	57,720,957	12/31/03
59.	The Moody Foundation (TX) http://www.moodyf.org/	57,621,881	12/31/04
60.	Verizon Foundation (NJ) http://foundation.verizon.com/	56,968,636	12/31/04
61.	Genentech Access To Care Foundation (CA) http://www.gene.com/gene/about/community/patients/access.jsp	56,804,289	12/31/04

©Thompson Publishing Group

Rank	Name/(State)	Total Giving	As of Fiscal Year End Date
62.	The JPMorgan Chase Foundation (NY) http://www.jpmorganchase.com/cm/cs?pagename=Chase/Href&urlname=jpmc/community/grants	56,786,083	12/31/04
63.	The Wallace Foundation (NY) http://www.wallacefoundation.org/WF/	56,665,282	12/31/05
64.	The Columbus Foundation and Affiliated Organizations (OH) http://www.columbusfoundation.org/GD/Templates/Pages/TCF/TCFDefault.aspx?page=1	54,554,071	12/31/04
65.	The Brown Foundation, Inc. (TX) http://www.brownfoundation.org/	52,849,201	06/30/05
66.	The Jonas Foundation (NJ)	52,101,100	07/31/04
67.	Ewing Marion Kauffman Foundation (MO) http://www.kauffman.org/	50,603,728	06/30/05
68.	Community Foundation for Greater Atlanta, Inc. (GA) http://www.atlcf.org/	49,998,065	06/30/05
69.	The James Irvine Foundation (CA) http://www.irvine.org/	49,407,820	12/31/04
70.	The Seattle Foundation (WA) http://www.seattlefoundation.org/	49,292,873	12/31/04
71.	Marin Community Foundation (CA) http://www.marincf.org/	49,224,806	06/30/04
72.	GE Foundation (CT) http://www.ge.com/foundation/index.html	49,177,477	12/31/04
73.	W. M. Keck Foundation (CA) http://www.wmkeck.org/	48,658,855	12/31/04
74.	Aspen Foundation, Inc. (NJ)	48,494,381	11/30/04
75.	AT&T Foundation (TX) http://att.sbc.com/gen/corporate-citizenship?pid=7736	48,159,537	12/31/04
76.	Fannie Mae Foundation (DC) http://www.fanniemaefoundation.org/	47,742,454	12/31/04
77.	The Baltimore Community Foundation (MD) http://www.bcf.org/	47,090,000	12/31/05
78.	Avon Foundation (NY) http://www.avoncompany.com/women/	45,974,681	12/31/05
79.	Daniels Fund (CO) http://www.danielsfund.org/	44,947,978	12/31/05
80.	Genzyme Charitable Foundation, Inc. (MA)	43,275,709	12/31/04
81.	Omaha Community Foundation (NE) http://www.omahafoundation.org/	43,224,293	12/31/05
82.	Johnson & Johnson Family of Companies Contribution Fund (NJ) http://www.jnj.com/community/contributions/index.htm	42,871,365	12/31/04
83.	The Lenfest Foundation, Inc. (PA) http://www.lenfestfoundation.org/	42,717,807	06/30/05

Rank	Name/(State)	Total Giving	As of Fiscal Year End Date
84.	Freeman Foundation (NY)	42,067,148	12/31/05
85.	The Minneapolis Foundation (MN) http://www.minneapolisfoundation.org/	41,788,667	03/31/05
86.	The Merck Company Foundation (NJ) http://www.merck.com/cr/company_profile/ philanthropy_at_merck/the_ merck_company_ foundation/home.html	41,736,724	12/31/04
87.	Overture Foundation (WI) http://www.overturefoundation.com/	41,589,701	12/31/04
88.	The San Diego Foundation (CA) http://www.sdfoundation.org/	41,106,000	06/30/05
89.	The Wachovia Foundation, Inc. (NC) http://www.wachovia.com/inside/page/0,,139_414_ 430,00.html	40,983,073	12/31/04
90.	The California Wellness Foundation (CA) http://www.tcwf.org/	40,505,102	12/31/04
91.	The Oregon Community Foundation (OR) http://www.ocf1.org/	40,478,757	12/31/05
92.	Horace W. Goldsmith Foundation (NY)	40,446,925	12/31/04
93.	Community Foundation of Middle Tennessee, Inc. (TN) http://www.cfmt.org/	39,949,273	12/31/04
94.	Greater Houston Community Foundation (TX) http://www.ghcf.org/	39,026,286	12/31/04
95.	The MBNA Foundation (DE) http://www.mbna.com/about/foundation/index.html	38,914,413	12/31/04
96.	Barr Foundation (MA) http://www.barrfoundation.org/index.html	37,642,680	12/31/05
97.	Lumina Foundation for Education, Inc. (IN) http://www.luminafoundation.org/	37,022,655	12/31/04
98.	Howard Heinz Endowment (PA) http://www.heinz.org/	36,557,675	12/31/04
99.	The UPS Foundation (GA) http://www.community.ups.com/philanthropy/main.html	36,552,454	12/31/04
100.	The Danforth Foundation (MO)	36,268,371	05/31/05

©2006, Foundation Center (foundationcenter.org). Reprinted with permission.

50 Largest Corporate Foundations by Total Giving

The following chart includes the 50 largest corporate foundations ranked by total giving. All figures are based on the most current audited financial data in the Foundation Center's database as of July 27, 2006.

Rank	Name/(State)	Total Giving	As of Fiscal Year End Date
1.	Wal-Mart Foundation (AR) http://www.walmartfoundation.org/wmstore/good- works/scripts/index.jsp	$154,537,406	01/31/05

©Thompson Publishing Group

Rank	Name/(State)	Total Giving	As of Fiscal Year End Date
2.	Aventis Pharmaceuticals Health Care Foundation (NJ)	114,668,984	12/31/04
3.	The Bank of America Charitable Foundation, Inc. (NC) http://www.bankofamerica.com/foundation/index.cfm?template=fd_funding	80,734,705	12/31/04
4.	Ford Motor Company Fund (MI) http://www.ford.com/en/goodWorks/fundingAnd-Grants/fordMotorCompanyFund/default.htm	77,916,903	12/31/04
5.	The Wells Fargo Foundation (CA) https://www.wellsfargo.com/about/charitable/index.jhtml?_requestid=7003	64,747,007	12/31/04
6.	ExxonMobil Foundation (TX) http://www.exxonmobil.com/Corporate/Citizenship/gcr_mainpage_categories.asp	63,660,965	12/31/05
7.	Citigroup Foundation (NY) http://www.citigroupfoundation.org/citigroup/corporate/foundation/	57,720,957	12/31/03
8.	Verizon Foundation (NJ) http://foundation.verizon.com/	56,968,636	12/31/04
9.	The JPMorgan Chase Foundation (NY) http://www.jpmorganchase.com/cm/cs?pagename=Chase/Href&urlname=jpmc/community/grants	56,786,083	12/31/04
10.	GE Foundation (CT) http://www.ge.com/foundation/index.html	49,177,477	12/31/04
11.	AT&T Foundation (TX) http://att.sbc.com/gen/corporate-citizenship?pid=7736	48,159,537	12/31/04
12.	Fannie Mae Foundation (DC) http://www.fanniemaefoundation.org/	47,742,454	12/31/04
13.	Avon Foundation (NY) http://www.avoncompany.com/women/	45,974,681	12/31/05
14.	Johnson & Johnson Family of Companies Contribution Fund (NJ) http://www.jnj.com/community/contributions/index.htm	42,871,365	12/31/04
15.	The Merck Company Foundation (NJ) http://www.merck.com/cr/company_profile/philanthropy_at_merck/the_ merck_company_foundation/home.html	41,736,724	12/31/04
16.	The Wachovia Foundation, Inc. (NC) http://www.wachovia.com/inside/page/0,,139_414_430,00.html	40,983,073	12/31/04
17.	The MBNA Foundation (DE) http://www.mbna.com/about/foundation/index.html	38,914,413	12/31/04
18.	The UPS Foundation (GA) http://www.community.ups.com/philanthropy/main.html	36,552,454	12/31/04
19.	Intel Foundation (OR) http://www.community.ups.com/philanthropy/main.html	34,561,326	12/31/04

Rank	Name/(State)	Total Giving	As of Fiscal Year End Date
20.	General Motors Foundation, Inc. (MI) http://www.gm.com/company/gmability/community/index.html	34,416,411	12/31/04
21.	MetLife Foundation (NY) http://www.metlife.com/Applications/Corporate/WPS/CDA/PageGenerator/0,,P284,00.html	29,746,890	12/31/05
22.	BP Foundation, Inc. (IL) http://www.bp.com/subsection.do?categoryId=9004440&contentId=7009902	28,536,711	12/31/04
23.	The Pfizer Foundation, Inc. (NY) http://www.pfizer.com/pfizer/subsites/philanthropy/index.jsp	27,464,145	12/31/04
24.	Eli Lilly and Company Foundation (IN) http://www.lilly.com/products/access/foundation.html	25,609,278	12/31/04
25.	The Procter & Gamble Fund (OH) http://www.pg.com/company/our_commitment/community.jhtml	25,389,729	06/30/05
26.	DaimlerChrysler Corporation Fund (MI) http://www2.daimlerchrysler.com/dccfund/	23,702,531	12/31/04
27.	Abbott Laboratories Fund (IL) http://www.abbott.com/global/url/content/en_US/40.80:80/general_content/General_Content_00070.htm	23,039,015	12/31/04
28.	Freddie Mac Foundation (VA) http://www.freddiemacfoundation.org/	22,790,389	12/31/04
29.	The Bristol-Myers Squibb Foundation, Inc. (NY) http://www.bms.com/aboutbms/founda/data/	21,955,431	12/31/04
30.	The PepsiCo Foundation, Inc. (NY) http://www.pepsico.com/PEP_Citizenship/Contributions/index.cfm	21,856,528	12/31/05
31.	The Prudential Foundation (NJ) http://www.prudential.com/productsAndServices/	21,818,030	12/31/04
32.	The Coca-Cola Foundation, Inc. (GA) http://www2.coca-cola.com/citizenship/foundation_coke.html	20,426,884	12/31/04
33.	State Farm Companies Foundation (IL) http://www.statefarm.com/about/part_spos/grants/foundati.asp	20,423,725	12/31/05
34.	General Mills Foundation (MN) http://www.generalmills.com/corporate/commitment/foundation.aspx	20,199,900	05/31/05
35.	American Express Foundation (NY) http://home3.americanexpress.com/corp/giving_back.asp	20,046,545	12/31/04
36.	U.S. Bancorp Foundation, Inc. (MN) http://www.usbank.com/cgi_w/cfm/about/community_relations/charit_giving.cfm	19,384,053	12/31/04

©Thompson Publishing Group

Rank	Name/(State)	Total Giving	As of Fiscal Year End Date
37.	NCC Charitable Foundation (OH) http://www.nationalcity.com/about/commurelations/default.asp	19,061,445	06/30/04
38.	3M Foundation (MN) http://solutions.3m.com/wps/portal/!ut/p/kcxml/04_Sj9SPykssy0xPLMnMz0vM0Q9KzYsPDdaP0I8yizeIDzbVL-8hwVAQAWqVLGQ!!	18,741,756	12/31/04
39.	The Medtronic Foundation (MN) http://www.medtronic.com/foundation/	18,526,625	04/30/05
40.	Merrill Lynch & Co. Foundation, Inc. (NJ) http://www.ml.com/philanthropy/	17,571,407	12/31/04
41.	Alcoa Foundation (PA) http://www.alcoa.com/global/en/community/info_page/foundation.asp	16,999,076	12/31/04
42.	Amgen Foundation, Inc. (CA) http://www.amgen.com/citizenship/foundation.html	16,279,383	12/31/04
43.	The Allstate Foundation (IL) http://www.allstate.com/Community/PageRender.asp?Page=foundation.html	15,983,966	12/31/05
44.	The Dow Chemical Company Foundation (MI) http://www.dow.com/about/corp/social/social.htm	15,953,729	12/31/05
45.	Emerson Charitable Trust (MO)	15,907,672	09/30/04
46.	Caterpillar Foundation (IL) http://www.cat.com/cda/layout?m=39201&x=7	15,407,405	12/31/04
47.	Simpson PSB Fund (CA)	15,297,005	12/31/04
48.	The Capital Group Companies Charitable Foundation (CA)	14,984,545	06/30/04
49.	Nationwide Foundation (OH) http://www.nationwide.com/nw/about-us/community-involvement/investing-in-people/index.htm?WT.svl=3#Nationwide%20Foundation	14,863,457	12/31/05
50.	Duke Energy Foundation (NC) http://www.duke-energy.com/community/foundations/duke%5Ffoundation/	14,739,126	12/31/04

©2006, Foundation Center (foundationcenter.org). Reprinted with permission.

25 Largest Community Foundations by Total Giving

The chart below includes the 25 largest community foundations ranked by total giving. All figures are based on the most current audited financial data in the Foundation Center's database as of May 1, 2006.

Rank	Name/(State)	Total Giving	As of Fiscal Year End Date
1.	The New York Community Trust (NY) http://www.nycommunitytrust.org/	$139,638,866	12/31/04
2.	Peninsula Community Foundation (CA) http://www.pcf.org/	110,910,875	12/31/04

Rank	Name/(State)	Total Giving	As of Fiscal Year End Date
3.	California Community Foundation (CA) http://www.calfund.org/	91,295,121	06/30/05
4.	The Community Foundation for the National Capital Region (DC) http://www.cfncr.org/	83,251,153	03/31/05
5.	Foundation for the Carolinas (NC) http://www.fftc.org/	82,821,824	12/31/04
6.	Community Foundation Silicon Valley (CA) http://www.cfsv.org/	75,366,593	06/30/05
7.	Communities Foundation of Texas, Inc. (TX) http://www.cftexas.org/	67,466,638	06/30/05
8.	The San Francisco Foundation (CA) http://www.sff.org/	64,392,830	06/30/04
9.	Boston Foundation, Inc. (MA) http://www.tbf.org/	64,092,145	06/30/05
10.	Greater Kansas City Community Foundation (MO) http://www.gkccf.org/	63,388,075	12/31/04
11.	The Cleveland Foundation (OH) http://www.clevelandfoundation.org/	62,432,351	12/31/04
12.	The Chicago Community Trust (IL) http://www.cct.org/index.html	61,677,060	09/30/04
13.	The Columbus Foundation and Affiliated Organizations (OH) http://www.columbusfoundation.org/GD/Templates/ Pages/ TCF/TCFDefault.aspx?page=1	54,554,071	12/31/04
14.	Community Foundation for Greater Atlanta, Inc. (GA) http://www.atlcf.org/	49,998,065	06/30/05
15.	The Seattle Foundation (WA) http://www.seattlefoundation.org/	49,292,873	12/31/04
16.	Marin Community Foundation (CA) http://www.marincf.org/	49,224,806	06/30/04
17.	The San Diego Foundation (CA) http://www.sdfoundation.org/	42,393,000	06/30/05
18.	The Minneapolis Foundation (MN) http://www.minneapolisfoundation.org/	41,788,667	03/31/05
19.	Community Foundation of Middle Tennessee, Inc. (TN) http://www.cfmt.org/	39,949,273	12/31/04
20.	Greater Houston Community Foundation (TX) http://www.ghcf.org/	39,026,286	12/31/04
21.	Community Foundation of Greater Memphis (TN) http://www.cfgm.org/	35,715,659	04/30/05
22.	The Oregon Community Foundation (OR) http://www.ocf1.org/	34,598,363	12/31/04
23.	The Greater Cincinnati Foundation (OH) http://www.greatercincinnatifdn.org/	33,817,396	12/31/04
24.	Oklahoma City Community Foundation, Inc. (OK) http://www.occf.org/occf/index.php	33,506,350	06/30/05
25.	Omaha Community Foundation (NE) http://www.omahafoundation.org/	32,155,318	12/31/04

©2006, Foundation Center (foundationcenter.org). Reprinted with permission.

©Thompson Publishing Group

Foundation Center Locations

You can visit a Foundation Center location or cooperating library to access hard copy and online nonprofit resource publications including the Foundation Directory and supplements, and FC-Search (CD-ROM and online database of U.S. foundations and corporations).

Headquarters:

New York
79 Fifth Ave./16th St.
New York, NY 10003-3076
212-620-4230
foundationcenter.org/newyork

Field Offices:

Atlanta
50 Hurt Plaza, Suite 150
Atlanta, GA 30303-2914
404-880-0094
foundationcenter.org/atlanta

Cleveland
1422 Euclid Ave., Suite 1600
Cleveland, OH 44115-2001
216-861-1934
foundationcenter.
  org/cleveland

San Francisco
312 Sutter St., Suite 606
San Francisco, CA 94108-4314
415-397-0902
foundationcenter.
  org/sanfrancisco

Washington, DC
1627 K St., N.W., Third Floor
Washington, DC 20006-1708
202-331-1400
foundationcenter.
  org/washington

Cooperating Collections

The Foundation Center Cooperating Collections are free funding information centers in libraries, community foundations and other nonprofit resource centers that provide a core collection of Foundation Center publications and a variety of supplementary materials and services in areas useful to grantseekers.

ALABAMA

Birmingham Public Library
Government Documents
2100 Park Place
Birmingham, AL 35203
205-226-3620

Huntsville Public Library
915 Monroe St.
Huntsville, AL 35801
256-532-5940

Mobile Public Library
West Regional Library
5555 Grelot Road
Mobile, AL 36609-3643
251-340-8555

**Auburn University at
  Montgomery Library**
74-40 East Drive
Montgomery, AL 36117-3596
334-244-3200

ALASKA

Consortium Library
3211 Providence Drive
Anchorage, AK 99508
907-786-1848

Juneau Public Library
Reference
292 Marine Way
Juneau, AK 99801
907-586-5267

ARIZONA

**Flagstaff City-Coconino
  County Public Library**
300 West Aspen Ave.
Flagstaff, AZ 86001
928-779-7670

Phoenix Public Library
Information Services
  Department
1221 N. Central
Phoenix, AZ 85004
602-262-4636

Tucson-Pima Library
101 N. Stone Ave.
Tucson, AZ 85701
520-791-4393

ARKANSAS

**University of Arkansas
– Fort Smith**
Boreham Library
5210 Grand Ave.
Fort Smith, AR 72913
479-788-7204

**Central Arkansas Library
System**
100 Rock St.
Little Rock, AR 72201
501-918-3000

CALIFORNIA

Kern County Library
Beale Memorial Library
701 Truxtun Ave.
Bakersfield, CA 93301

Humboldt Area Foundation
Rooney Resource Center
373 Indianola
Bayside, CA 95524
707-442-2993

**Ventura County Community
Foundation**
Resource Center for Nonprofit
Organizations
1317 Del Norte Road, Suite 150
Camarillo, CA 93010
805-988-0196

**Solano Community
Foundation**
1261 Travis Blvd., Suite 320
Fairfield, CA 94533
707-399-3846

**Fresno Nonprofit
Advancement Council**
1752 L St.
Fresno, CA 93721
559-264-1513

**Center For Nonprofit
Management In Southern
California**
Nonprofit Resource Library
Center for Healthy
Communities
1000 N. Alameda St.
Los Angeles, CA 90012
213-687-9511

**Southern California Library
For Social Studies And
Research**
6120 S. Vermont Ave.
Los Angeles, CA 90044
323-759-6063

Los Angeles Public Library
Mid-Valley Regional Branch
Library
16244 Nordhoff St.
North Hills, CA 91343
818-895-3654

Flintridge Foundation
Philanthropy Resource Library
1040 Lincoln Ave., Suite 100
Pasadena, CA 91103
626-449-0839

**High Desert Resource
Network**
10178 I Ave., Suite C
Phelan, CA 92329
760-949-2930

**Shasta Regional Community
Foundation's Center For
Nonprofit Resources**
Building C, Suite A
2280 Benton Drive
Redding, CA 96003
530-244-1219

Richmond Public Library
325 Civic Center Plaza
Richmond, CA 94804
510-620-6561

Riverside Public Library
3581 Mission Inn Ave.
Riverside, CA 92501
909-826-5201

Nonprofit Resource Center
828 I St., 2nd Floor
Sacramento, CA 95814
916-264-2772

San Diego Foundation
Funding Information Center
1420 Kettner Blvd., Suite 500
San Diego, CA 92101
619-235-2300

**Foundation Center Office
And Library**
312 Sutter St., Suite 606
San Francisco, CA 94108
415-397-0902

**Compasspoint Nonprofit
Services**
Nonprofit Development
Library
1922 The Alameda, Suite 212
San Jose, CA 95126
408-248-9505

Los Angeles Public Library
San Pedro Regional Branch
931 S. Gaffey St.
San Pedro, CA 90731
310-548-7779

**Volunteer Center of Orange
County**
Nonprofit Management
Assistance Center
1901 East 4th St., Suite 100
Santa Ana, CA 92705
714-953-5757

**Santa Barbara Public
Library**
40 E. Anapamu St.
Santa Barbara, CA 93101-1019
805-962-7653

Santa Monica Public Library
1324 Fifth St.
Santa Monica, CA 90401
310-458-8600

Sonoma County Library
3rd & E St.
Santa Rosa, CA 95404
707-545-0831

Seaside Branch Library
550 Harcourt Ave.
Seaside, CA 93955
831-899-2055

 ©Thompson Publishing Group

Sierra Nonprofit Support Center
39 N. Washington St. #F
Sonora, CA 95370
209-533-1093

COLORADO

El Pomar Nonprofit Resource Center
Penrose Library
20 N. Cascade
Colorado Springs, CO 80903
719-531-6333

Denver Public Library
General Reference
10 W. 14th Ave. Parkway
Denver, CO 80204
720-865-1111

Durango Public Library
1188 E. Second Ave.
Durango, CO 81301
970-375-3380

Weld Library District
Farr Branch Library
1939 61st Ave.
Greeley, CO 80634
970-506-8518

Pueblo City-County Library District
100 E. Abriendo Ave.
Pueblo, CO 81004-4232
719-562-5600

CONNECTICUT

Greenwich Public Library
101 W. Putnam Ave.
Greenwich, CT 06830
203-622-7900

Hartford Public Library
500 Main St.
Hartford, CT 06103
860-695-6292

New Haven Free Public Library
Reference Dept.
133 Elm St.
New Haven, CT 06510-2057
203-946-7431

Westport Public Library
20 Jesup Road
Arnold Bernhard Plaza
Westport, CT 06880
203-291-4850

DELAWARE

University of Delaware
Hugh Morris Library
181 S. College Ave.
Newark, DE 19717-5267
302-831-2432

DISTRICT OF COLUMBIA

Foundation Center Office And Library
1627 K St., N.W., Third Floor
Washington, DC 20006
202-331-1400

FLORIDA

Bartow Public Library
2150 S. Broadway Ave.
Bartow, FL 33830
863-534-0131

Volusia County Library Center
City Island
105 E. Magnolia Ave.
Daytona Beach, FL 32114-4484
386-257-6036

Nova Southeastern University
Research and Information Technology Library
3100 College Ave.
Fort Lauderdale, FL 33314
954-262-4613

Indian River Community College
Learning Resources Center
3209 Virginia Ave.
Fort Pierce, FL 34981-5596
772-462-7600

Jacksonville Public Libraries
Nonprofit Resource Center
303 N. Laura St.
Jacksonville, FL 32202
904-630-2665

Miami-Dade Public Library
Humanities/Social Science Dept.
101 W. Flagler St.
Miami, FL 33130
305-375-5575

Orange County Library System
Social Sciences Department
101 E. Central Blvd.
Orlando, FL 32801
407-425-4694

Selby Public Library
Reference
1331 First St.
Sarasota, FL 34236
941-861-1100

State Library of Florida
R.A. Gray Building
Tallahassee, FL 32399-0250
850-245-6600

Hillsborough County Public Library Cooperative
John F. Germay Public Library
900 N. Ashley Drive
Tampa, FL 33602
813-273-3652

Community Foundation of Palm Beach & Martin Counties
Temporarily relocated due to Hurricane Wilma damage at:
319 Clematis St.
Suite 900
West Palm Beach, FL 33401
561-659-6800

GEORGIA

Atlanta Field Office and Library
Suite 150, Grand Lobby
Hurt Building, 50 Hurt Plaza
Atlanta, GA 30303-2914
404-880-0094

Coastal Georgia Nonprofit Center
1311 Union St.
Brunswick, GA 31520
912-265-1850

Hall County Library System
127 Main St. N.W.
Gainesville, GA 30501
770-532-3311

Methodist Home
Rumford Center
304 Pierce Ave., 1st floor
Macon, GA 31204
478-751-2202

**Thomas County Public
Library**
201 N. Madison St.
Thomasville, GA 31792
229-225-5252

HAWAII

University of Hawaii
Hamilton Library
General/Humanities/Soc.
Science Reference Dept.
2550 The Mall
Honolulu HI 96822
808-956-7214

IDAHO

Funding Information Center
Boise Public Library
715 S. Capitol Blvd.
Boise, ID 83702
208-384-4024

Caldwell Public Library
1010 Dearborn St.
Caldwell, ID 83605
208-459-3242

Marshall Public Library
113 South Garfield
Pocatello, ID 83204
208-232-1263

ILLINOIS

Carbondale Public Library
405 West Main
Carbondale, IL 62901-2995
618-457-0354

Donors Forum of Chicago
208 South LaSalle, Suite 735
Chicago, IL 60604
312-578-0175

Evanston Public Library
1703 Orrington Ave.
Evanston, IL 60201
847-866-0300

**John Wood Community
College**
1301 S. 48th St.
Quincy, IL 62305
217-224-6500

Rock Island Public Library
401 19th St.
Rock Island, IL 61201-8143
309-732-7323

**Central Illinois Nonprofit
Resources Center**
Brookens Library
University of Illinois at
Springfield
One University Plaza, MS BRK
140
Springfield, IL 62703-5407
217-206-6633

INDIANA

**Evansville Vanderburgh
County Public Library**
200 S.E. Martin Luther King Jr.
Blvd.
Evansville, IN 47713
812-428-8218

Allen County Public Library
200 E. Berry St.
Fort Wayne, IN 46802
260-421-1238

**Indianapolis-Marion County
Public Library**
202 N. Alabama
Indianapolis, IN 46206
317-269-1700

Muncie Public Library
2005 S. High St.
Muncie, IN 47302
765-747-8204

Vigo County Public Library
1 Library Square
Terre Haute, IN 47807
812-232-1113

**The Christopher Center For
Library and Information
Resources**
Valparaiso University
1410 Chapel Drive
Valparaiso, IN 46383
219-464-5364

IOWA

Cedar Rapids Public Library
Foundation Center Collection
500 First St. S.E.
Cedar Rapids, IA 52401
319-398-5123

**Council Bluffs Public
Library**
400 Willow Ave.
Council Bluffs, IA 51503
712-323-7553

**Southwestern Community
College**
Learning Resource Center
1501 W. Townline Road
Creston, IA 50801
641-782-7081

Des Moines Public Library
100 Locust
Des Moines, IA 50309-1791
515-283-4152

Sioux City Public Library
529 Pierce St.
Sioux City, IA 51101-1202
712-255-2933

KANSAS

Pioneer Memorial Library
375 W. 4th St.
Colby 67701
785-462-4470

Dodge City Public Library
1001 2nd Ave.
Dodge City, KS 67801
316-225-0248

Kearny County Library
101 E. Prairie
Lakin, KS 67860
620-355-6674

Salina Public Library
301 W. Elm
Salina, KS 67401
785-825-4624

©Thompson Publishing Group

Topeka and Shawnee County Public Library
1515 S.W. 10th Ave.
Topeka, KS 66604
785-580-4400

Wichita Public Library
223 S. Main St.
Wichita, KS 67202
316-261-8500

KENTUCKY

Western Kentucky University
Helm-Cravens Library
110 Helm Library
Bowling Green, KY 42101-3576
270-745-6163

Lexington Public Library
140 E. Main St.
Lexington, KY 40507-1376
859-231-5520

Louisville Free Public Library
301 York St.
Louisville, KY 40203
502-574-1617

Puluaski County Public Library
107 N. Main St.
Somerset, KY 42501
606-679-8401

LOUISIANA

The Rapides Foundation
Community Development Works Program
1101 4th St.
Alexandria, LA 71309-0028
318-443-7880

East Baton Rouge Parish Library
River Center Branch Grants Collection
120 St. Louis
Baton Rouge, LA 70802
225-389-4967

Beauregard Parish Library
205 S. Washington Ave.
De Ridder, LA 70634
337-463-6217

Ouachita Parish Public Library
1800 Stubbs Ave.
Monroe, LA 71201
318-327-1490

New Orleans Public Library
Business & Science Division
219 Loyola Ave.
New Orleans, LA 70112
504-596-2580

Shreve Memorial Library
424 Texas St.
Shreveport, LA 71120-1523
318-226-5894

MAINE

The Maine Philanthropy Center
University of Southern Maine Library
314 Forrest Ave.
Portland, ME 04104-9301
207-780-5029

MARYLAND

Enoch Pratt Free Library
Social Science & History
400 Cathedral St.
Baltimore, MD 21201
410-396-5320

MASSACHUSETTS

Associated Grant Makers
55 Court St., Room 520
Boston, MA 02108
617-426-2606

Boston Public Library
Soc. Sci. Reference
700 Boylston St.
Boston, MA 02116
617-536-5400

Berkshire Athenaeum
1 Wendell Ave.
Pittsfield, MA 02201-6385
413-499-9480

Western Massachusetts Funding Resource Center
65 Elliot St.
Springfield, MA 01101-1730
413-452-0697

Worcester Public Library
Grants Resource Center
3 Salem Square
Worcester, MA 01608
508-799-1654

MICHIGAN

Alpena County Library
211 N. First St.
Alpena, MI 49707
989-356-6188

University of Michigan – Ann Arbor
Graduate Library
Reference & Research Services Department
Ann Arbor, MI 48109-1205
734-763-1539

Willard Public Library
Nonprofit and Funding Resource Collections
7 W. Van Buren St.
Battle Creek, MI 49017
269-968-8166

Purdy/Kresge Library
134 Purdy/Kresge Library
Wayne State University
Detroit, MI 48202
313-577-6424

Michigan State University Libraries
Main Library Funding Center
100 Library
East Lansing, MI 48824-1049
517-432-6123

Farmington Community Library
32737 W. 12 Mile Road
Farmington Hills, MI 48334
248-553-0300

Flint Public Library
1026 E. Kearsley St.
Flint, MI 48502-1994
810-232-7111

Grand Rapids Public Library
Reference Department
111 Library St. N.E.
Grand Rapids, MI 49503-3268
616-988-5400

Michigan Technological University
Corporate Services
ATDC Bldg, Suite 200
1402 E. Sharon Ave.
Houghton MI 49931-1295
906-487-2228

West Shore Community College Library
3000 N. Stiles Road
Scottville, MI 49454-0277
231-845-6211

Traverse Area District Library
610 Woodmere Ave.
Traverse City, MI 49686
231-932-8500

MINNESOTA

Brainerd Public Library
416 S. Fifth St.
Brainerd, MN 56401
218-829-5574

Duluth Public Library
520 W. Superior St.
Duluth, MN 55802
218-723-3802

Southwest State University
University Library
North Highway 23
Marshall, MN 56253
507-537-6108

Minneapolis Public Library
300 Nicollet Mall
Minneapolis, MN 55401
612-630-6000

Rochester Public Library
101 2nd St. S.E.
Rochester, MN 55904-3777
507-285-8002

St. Paul Public Library
90 W. Fourth St.
St. Paul, MN 55102
651-266-7000

MISSISSIPPI

Library of Hattiesburg, Petal And Forrest County
329 Hardy St.
Hattiesburg, MS 39401-3824
601-582-4461

Jackson/Hinds Library System
300 N. State St.
Jackson, MS 39201
601-968-5803

MISSOURI

Council on Philanthropy
University of Missouri – Kansas City
4747 Troost, Room 207
Kansas City, MO 64110
816-235-6259

Kansas City Public Library
14 W. 10th St.
Kansas City, MO 64105-1702
816-701-3541

St. Louis Public Library
1301 Olive St.
St. Louis, MO 63103
314-241-2288

Springfield-Greene County Library
4653 S. Campbell
Springfield, MO 65810
417-874-8110

MONTANA

Fallon County Library
6 W. Fallon Ave.
Baker, MT 59313-1037
Phone: 406)778-7160

Montana State University – Billings
Library – Special Collections
1500 N. 30th St.
Billings, MT 59101-0245
406-657-2262

Bozeman Public Library
220 E. Lamme
Bozeman, MT 59715
406-582-2402

Lincoln County Public Libraries
Libby Public Library
220 W. 6th St.
Libby, MT 59923
406-293-2778

University of Montana
Maureen & Mike Mansfield Library
32 Campus Drive, #9936
Missoula, MT 59812-9936
406-243-6800

NEBRASKA

Butler Memorial Library
621 Penn St.
Cambridge, NE 69022
308-697-3836

University of Nebraska-Lincoln
225 Love Library
14th & R Sts.
Lincoln, NE 68588-2848
402-472-2848

Omaha Public Library
Social Sciences Department
215 S. 15th St.
Omaha, NE 68102
402-444-4826

NEVADA

Great Basin College Library
1500 College Parkway
Elko, NV 89801
775-753-2222

Clark County Library
1401 E. Flamingo
Las Vegas, NV 89119
702-507-3400

Washoe County Library
301 S. Center St.
Reno, NV 89501

NEW HAMPSHIRE

Concord Public Library
45 Green St.
Concord, NH 03301
603-225-8670

Herbert H. Lamson Library
Plymouth State College
Plymouth, NH 03264
603-535-2258

©Thompson Publishing Group

NEW JERSEY

Free Public Library of Elizabeth
11 S. Broad St.
Elizabeth, NJ 07202
908-354-6060

County College of Morris Learning Resources Center
214 Center Grove Rd.
Randolph, NJ 07869
973-328-5296

New Jersey State Library
Governmental Reference Services
185 W. State St.
Trenton, NJ 08625-0520
609-292-6220

Warren County Community College
475 Route 57 West
Washington, NJ 07882
908-835-2336

NEW MEXICO

Albuquerque/Bernalillo County Library System
501 Copper Ave. N.W.
Albuquerque, NM 87102
505-768-5141

New Mexico State Library
Information Services
1209 Camino Carlos Rey
Santa Fe, NM 87507
505-476-9702

NEW YORK

New York State Library
Humanities Reference
Cultural Education Center
6th Floor
Empire State Plaza
Albany, NY 12230
518-474-5355

Brooklyn Public Library
Social Sciences/Philosophy Division
Grand Army Plaza
Brooklyn, NY 11238
718-230-2122

Buffalo & Erie County Public Library
Business, Science and Technology Dept.
1 Lafayette Square
Buffalo, NY 14203-1887
716-858-7097

Southeast Steuben County Library
300 Nasser Civic Center Plaza
Corning, NY 14830
607-936-3713

Sachem Public Library
150 Holbrook Road
Holbrook, NY 11741
631-588-5024

Huntington Public Library
338 Main St.
Huntington, NY 11743
631-427-5165

Queens Borough Public Library
Social Sciences Division
89-11 Merrick Blvd.
Jamaica, NY 11432
718-990-0700

Levittown Public Library
1 Bluegrass Lane
Levittown, NY 11756
516-731-5728

Foundation Center Office and Library
79 Fifth Ave.
2nd Floor
New York, NY 10003-3076
212-620-4230

Adriance Memorial Library
Special Services Department
93 Market St.
Poughkeepsie, NY 12601
845-485-3445

The Riverhead Free Library
330 Court St.
Riverhead, NY 11901
631-727-3228

Rochester Public Library
Social Sciences
115 South Ave.
Rochester, NY 14604
585-428-8120

Onondaga County Public Library
447 S. Salina St.
Syracuse, NY 13202-2494
315-435-1900

Utica Public Library
303 Genesee St.
Utica, NY 13501
315-735-2279

White Plains Public Library
100 Martine Ave.
White Plains, NY 10601
914-422-1480

Yonkers Public Library
Riverfront Library
One Larkin Center
Yonkers, NY 10701
914-337-1500

NORTH CAROLINA

Community Foundation of Western North Carolina
Pack Memorial Library
67 Haywood St.
Asheville, NC 28801
828-254-4960

The Duke Endowment
100 N. Tryon St., Suite 3500
Charlotte, NC 28202-4012
704-376-0291

Durham County Public Library
300 North Roxboro
Durham, NC 27702
919-560-0100

Cameron Village Regional Library
Wake County Public Libraries
1930 Clark Ave.
Raleigh, NC 27605
919-856-6710

New Hanover County Public Library
201 Chestnut St.
Wilmington, NC 28401-3942
910-798-6301

Forsyth County Public Library
660 W. Fifth St.
Winston-Salem, NC 27101
336-727-2264

NORTH DAKOTA

Bismarck Public Library
515 N. Fifth St.
Bismarck, ND 58501-4081
701-222-6410

Fargo Public Library
102 N. Third St.
Fargo, ND 58102
701-241-1491

Minot Public Library
516 Second Ave. S.W.
Minot, ND 58701-3792
701-852-1045

OHIO

Akron-Summit County Public Library
60 S. High St.
Akron, OH 44326
330-643-9000

Stark County District Library
715 Market Ave. N.
Canton, OH 44702
330-452-0665

Public Library of Cincinnati & Hamilton County
Grants Resource Center
800 Vine St., Library Square
Cincinnati, OH 45202-2071
513-369-6000

Foundation Center Office and Library
1422 Euclid Ave., Suite 1600
Cleveland, OH 44115
216-861-1934

Columbus Metropolitan Library
Business and Technology Dept.
96 S. Grant Ave.
Columbus, OH 43215
614-645-2590

Dayton Metro Library
Grants Information Center
215 E. Third St.
Dayton, OH 45402
937-227-9500 x322

Elyria Public Library – West River Branch
1194 W. River Road N.
Elyria, OH 44035
440-324-9827

Mansfield/Richland County Public Library
42 W. 3rd St.
Mansfield, OH 44902
419-521-3100

Portsmouth Public Library
1220 Gallia St.
Portsmouth, OH 45662
740-354-5688

Toledo-Lucas County Public Library
Social Sciences Department
325 Michigan St.
Toledo, OH 43612
419-259-5209

Public Library of Youngstown & Mahoning County
305 Wick Ave.
Youngstown, OH 44503
330-744-8636

OKLAHOMA

Oklahoma City University
Dulaney Browne Library
2501 N. Blackwelder
Oklahoma City, OK 73106
405-521-5822

Tulsa City-County Library
400 Civic Center
Tulsa, OK 74103
918-596-7977

OREGON

University of Oregon – Knight Library
1501 Kincaid
Eugene, OR 97403
541-346-3053

Oregon Institute of Technology
Library
3201 Campus Drive
Klamath Falls, OR 97601-8801
541)-885-1000

Jackson County Library Services
205 South Central Ave.
Medford, OR 97501
541-774-8689

Multnomah County Library
Government Documents
801 S.W. 10th Ave.
Portland, OR 97205
503-988-5123

Oregon State Library
State Library Building
250 Winter St. N.E.
Salem, OR 97310-3950
503-378-4277

PENNSYLVANIA

Northampton Community College
Paul and Harriett Mack Library
3835 Green Pond Road
Bethlehem, PA 18017
610-861-5360

Erie County Library
160 E. Front St.
Erie, PA 16507
814-451-6927

Dauphin County Library System
East Shore Area Library
4501 Ethel St.
Harrisburg, PA 17109
717-652-9380

Hazleton Area Public Library
55 N. Church St.
Hazleton, PA 18201
570-454-2961

Lancaster Public Library
125 N. Duke St.
Lancaster, PA 17602
717-394-2651

©Thompson Publishing Group

Free Library of Philadelphia
Regional Foundation Center
1901 Vine St., 2nd Floor
Philadelphia, PA 19103-1189
215-686-5423

**Johnson Memorial United
Methodist Church**
3117 Longshore Ave.
Philadelphia, PA 19149
215-338-4487

**Carnegie Library of
Pittsburgh – Downtown &
Business**
612 Smithfield St.
Pittsburgh, PA 15222
412-281-7143

**Nonprofit & Community
Assistance Center**
1151 Oak St.
Pittston, PA 18640
570-655-5581

Reading Public Library
100 S. Fifth St.
Reading, PA 19602
610-655-6355

James V. Brown Library
19 E. Fourth St.
Williamsport, PA 17701
570-326-0536

Martin Library
159 Market St.
York, PA 17401
717-846-5300

PUERTO RICO

**Universidad Del Sagrado
Corazon**
M.M.T. Guevara Library
Santurce, PR 00914
787-728-1515 x4354

RHODE ISLAND

Providence Public Library
150 Empire St.
Providence, RI 02903
401-455-8088

SOUTH CAROLINA

Anderson County Library
300 N. McDuffie St.
Anderson, SC 29622
864-260-4500

Charleston County Library
68 Calhoun St.
Charleston, SC 29401
843-805-6930

**South Carolina State
Library**
1500 Senate St.
Columbia, SC 29211
803-734-8666

**Greenville County Library
System**
25 Heritage Green Place
Greenville, SC 29601-2034
864-242-5000

**Spartanburg County Public
Libraries**
151 S. Church St.
Spartanburg, SC 29301
864-596-3500

SOUTH DAKOTA

Dakota State University
Nonprofit Management
Institute
Nonprofit Grants Assistance
820 N. Washington
Madison, SD 57042
605-782-3089

South Dakota State Library
800 Governors Drive
Pierre, SD 57501-2294
605-773-3131
1-800-423-6665 (within SD-

Black Hills State University
E.Y. Berry Library-Learning
Center
1200 University St. Unit 9676
Spearfish, SD 57799-9676
605-642-6833

TENNESSEE

**United Way of Greater
Chatanooga**
Center for Nonprofits
630 Market St.
Chattanooga, TN 37402
423-265-0514

Knox County Public Library
500 W. Church Ave.
Knoxville, TN 37902
865-215-8751

**Memphis & Shelby County
Public Library**
3030 Poplar Ave.
Memphis, TN 38111
901-415-2734

Nashville Public Library
615 Church St.
Nashville, TN 37219
615-862-5800

TEXAS

Amarillo Area Foundation
Grants Center
801 S. Fillmore
Amarillo, TX 79101
806-376-4521

**Hogg Foundation For Mental
Health**
Regional Foundation Library
3001 Lake Austin Blvd.
Austin, TX 78703
512-471-5041
1-888-404-4336

Beaumont Public Library
801 Pearl St.
Beaumont, TX 77704-3827
409-838-6606

**Corpus Christi Public
Library**
Funding Information Center
805 Comanche St.
Corpus Christi, TX 78401
361-880-7000

Dallas Public Library
Urban Information
1515 Young St.
Dallas, TX 75201
214-670-1400

Southwest Border Nonprofit Resource Center
1201 W. University Drive
Edinburgh, TX 78539-2999
956-384-5920

University of Texas at El Paso
Community Non-Profit Grant Library
500 W. University
Benedict Hall Room 103
El Paso, TX 79968-0547
915-747-7969

Funding Information Center of Fort Worth
329 S. Henderson
Fort Worth, TX 76104
817-334-0228

Houston Public Library
Bibliographic Information Center
500 McKinney
Houston, TX 77002
832-393-1313

Laredo Public Library
Nonprofit Management and Volunteer Center
1120 E. Calton Road
Laredo, TX 78041
956-795-2400

Longview Public Library
222 W. Cotton St.
Longview, TX 75601
903-237-1350

Lubbock Area Foundation Inc.
1655 Main St., Suite 209
Lubbock, TX 79401
806-762-8061

Nonprofit Resource Center of Texas
7404 Highway 90 W.
San Antonio, TX 78212-8270
210-227-4333

Nonprofit Development Center of United Way of Tyler/Smith County
4000 Southpark Drive
Tyler, TX 75703
903-581-6376

Waco-Mclennan County Library
1717 Austin Ave.
Waco, TX 76701
254-750-5941

Nonprofit Management Center of Wichita Falls
2301 Kell Blvd. Suite 218
Wichita Falls, TX 76308
940-322-4961

UTAH

Grand County Public Library
257 E. Center St.
Moab, UT 84532
435-259-5421

Salt Lake City Public Library
210 E. 400 S.
Salt Lake City, Utah 84111
801-524-8200

Utah Nonprofits Association
175 S. Main St., Suite 750
Salt Lake City, Utah 84111
801-596-1800

VERMONT

Ilsley Public Library
75 Main St.
Middlebury, VT 05753
802-388-4095

Vermont Department of Libraries
Reference & Law Info. Services
109 State St.
Montpelier, VT 05609
802-828-3261

VIRGINIA

Washington County Public Library
205 Oak Hill St.
Abingdon, VA 24210
276-676-6222

Fairfax County Public Library
12000 Government Center Parkway
Suite 329
Fairfax, VA 22035
703-324-3100

Hampton Public Library
4207 Victoria Blvd.
Hampton, VA 23669
757-727-1314

Richmond Public Library
Business, Science & Technology
101 E. Franklin St.
Richmond, VA 23219
804-646-7223

Roanoke City Public Library System
Main Library
706 S. Jefferson St.
Roanoke, VA 24016
540-853-2471

WASHINGTON

Mid-Columbia Library
Reference Department
1620 S. Union St.
Kennewick, WA 99336
509-783-7878

King County Library System
Redmond Regional Library
Nonprofit & Philanthropy Resource Center
15990 N.E. 85th
Redmond, WA 98052
425-885-1861

Seattle Public Library
The Fundraising Resource Center
1000 4th Ave.
Seattle, WA 98104
206-386-4636

Spokane Public Library
Funding Information Center
906 W. Main Ave.
Spokane, WA 99201
509-444-5300

Tacoma Library
University of Washington
1900 Commerce St.
Tacoma, WA 98403-3100
253-692-4440

©Thompson Publishing Group

WEST VIRGINIA

Kanawha County Public Library
123 Capitol St.
Charleston, WV 25301
304-343-4646

West Virginia University At Parkersburg
Library
300 Campus Drive
Parkersburg, WV 26104-8647
304-876-5424

Shepherd University
Ruth A. Scarborough Library
King St.
Shepherdstown, WV 25443-3210
304-424-8000

WISCONSIN

University of Wisconsin-Madison
Memorial Library, Grants Information Center
728 State St.
Madison, WI 53706
608-262-3242

Marquette University Memorial Library
Funding Information Center
1355 W. Wisconsin Ave.
Milwaukee WI 53201-3141
414-288-1515

University of Wisconsin-Stevens Point
Library – Foundation Collection
900 Reserve St.
Stevens Point, WI 54481-3897
715-346-2540

WYOMING

Laramie County Community College
Instructional Resource Center
1400 E. College Drive
Cheyenne, WY 82007-3299
307-778-1206

Campbell County Public Library
2101 4-J Road
Gillette, WY 82718
307-687-0115

Teton County Library
125 Virginian Lane
Jackson, WY 83001
307-733-2164

Sheridan County Fulmer Public Library
335 W. Alger St.
Sheridan, WY 82801
307-674-8585

Funding Resources Available to Grantseekers

Federal Grants

Grants.gov – This Web site hosts 900 grant programs administered by 26 federal grant-making agencies that collectively award more than $400 billion in grants each year. Grants.gov is considered the one-stop Web site for finding federal government grant funding announcements. In my opinion, Grants.gov has replaced the Federal Register when it comes to finding grant programs quickly. Once you pull up this Web site on your Internet browser, look under **Quick Links** and click on **Grant E-mail Alerts**. It's a quick and easy signup process: Select **Receive Grant Opportunity E-mail Alerts** and then **All Grant Notices**. Fig. 9-1 shows how the Web page will look when you open the home page.

FIG. 9-1

On the **Subscription Services** page (Fig. 9-2), enter your e-mail address and click enter to start receiving federal grant funding alerts, free of charge, in your e-mail inbox.

FIG. 9-2

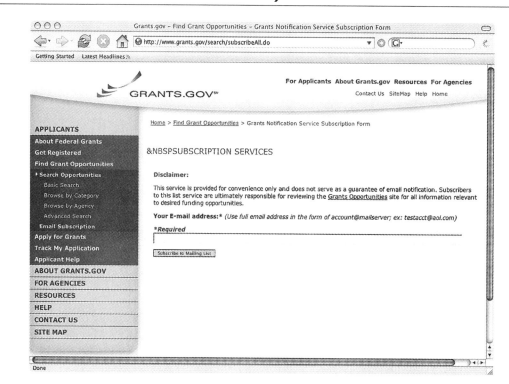

©Thompson Publishing Group

Under the **Find Grant Opportunities** link on the left side of the main page, you can also use Grants.gov to search for federal grant programs. To start your search, click on **Basic Search** and then type one or two words such as social services, homeless, housing, charter school, or youth development in the "keyword search" box. Think about what your organization does or provides and break the services down into one or two word search terms. Fig. 9-3 shows what the Grants.gov search screen looks like:

FIG. 9-3

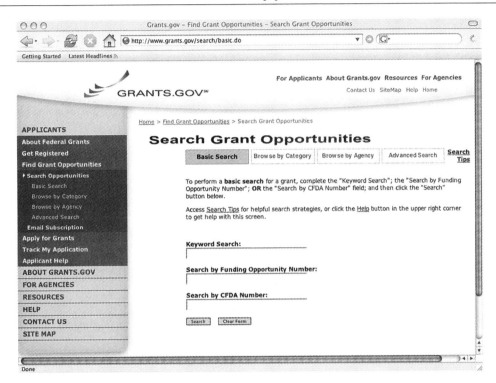

Thompson.com – Grantseekers of all kinds (i.e. state, local and Indian tribal governments, nonprofit or educational organizations, faith-based and community groups) can benefit from a host of grants-related publications from Thompson Publishing Group. There is Local/State Funding Report, a weekly newsletter that provides up-to-date information on grant opportunities; Guide to Federal Funding for Governments & Nonprofits that offers detailed descriptions of hundreds of federal grant programs; the Federal Grants Management Handbook, that provides grant recipients with all the information they will need to successfully manage their federal grants; as well as the Single Audit Information Service and a number of other grant-related publications. These publications can be found at http://www.thompson.com/public/library.jsp?cat=GRANT.

Foundation and Corporate Grants
Foundationcenter.org (paid subscription required to access Online Foundation Directory) – The Foundation Center is the nation's leading authority on philanthropy and is dedicated to

Remember, even if you find a federal grant funding announcement and the deadline has passed, you can always call or e-mail the agency contact person (information listed in announcement) to inquire about the likelihood of more grant funding competitions in this or the next federal fiscal year (Oct. 1 to Sept. 30).

serving grantseekers, grantmakers, researchers, policymakers, the media and the general public. Its Web site is full of foundation and corporate grantmaker information. From its home page (Fig. 9-4), if you already know the name of a foundation, you can look it up without being a paid subscriber by simply typing in the name and, if known, the state.

Fig. 9-4

©2006, Foundation Center (foundationcenter.org). Reprinted with permission.

While you won't see the same detailed descriptive information on a foundation using the free search tool, you will find its full contact information. The free search tool will also allow you to click on a link to view the foundation's IRS Form 990, which contains the foundation's most recent financial data and a complete list of all the grants it has awarded over the past year.

©Thompson Publishing Group

For example, Fig. 9-5 shows the information that is made available using the search tool for the Charles Stewart Mott Foundation, one of the nation's largest foundations.

FIG. 9-5

©2006, Foundation Center (foundationcenter.org). Reprinted with permission.

The Foundation Center's **Funding Directory Online** houses a database of 250,000 searchable IRS Form 990s, 80,000 funder profiles and a half million recently awarded grants. The center offers five subscription plans for **Funding Directory Online**, ranging from basic to professional, which provide varying levels of search capability and information access.

There are several ways to search the Foundation Center's funding directory. For example, you can enter the project's state in the **Geographic Focus** field and the project's focus (i.e., youth, animals, health or historic preservation) in the **Text Search** field.

Then select **Sort By: Total Giving** and **Descending**. Doing this will list the largest grant-makers first. Fig. 9-6 displays this "find quick money" search technique.

Fig. 9-6

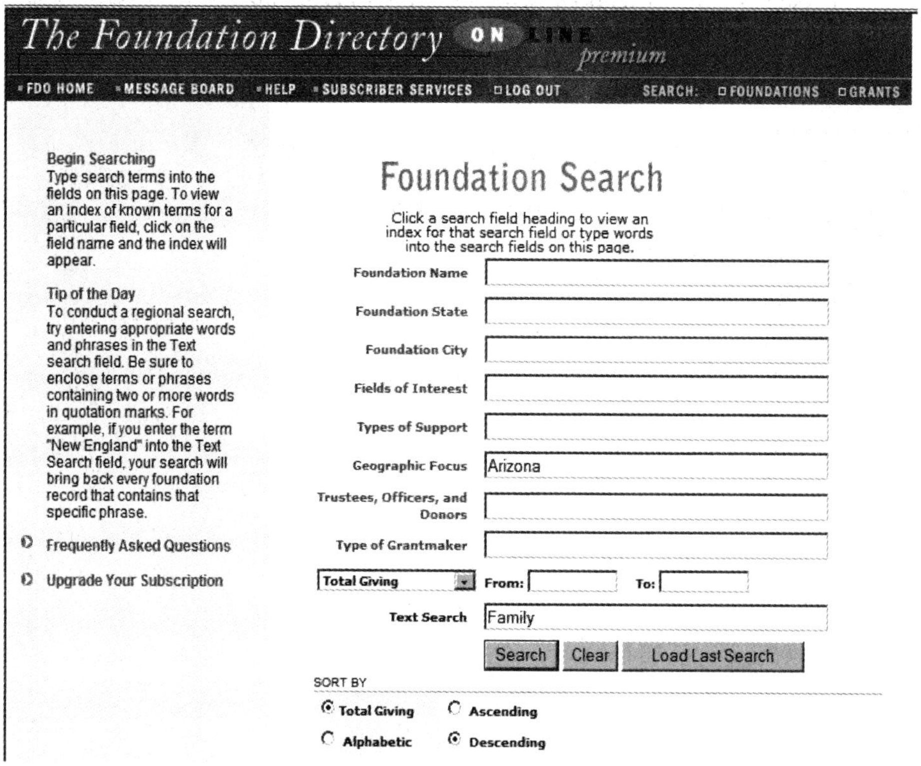

©2006, Foundation Center (foundationcenter.org). Reprinted with permission.

Grants for Education Organizations

Grantsalert.com (free public access) – This Web site provides teachers, schools and re-lated organizations with free access to up-to-date announcements of corporate, foundation, state and federal education funding opportunities. You can also sign up for a free e-mail alert to receive weekly grant announcement updates. At the top of the home page (see Fig. 9-7), you can scroll through the most recent grant funding opportunities.

©Thompson Publishing Group

Fig. 9-7

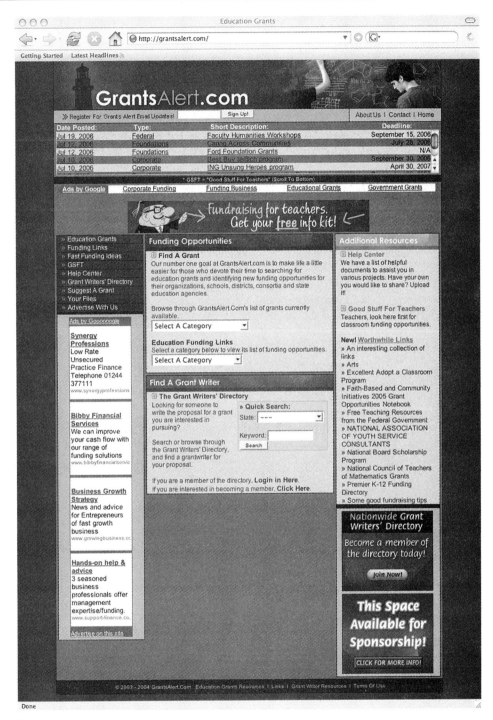

©2006, GrantsAlert.com. Reprinted with permission.

Other Sources

Fundsnetservices.com (Fig. 9-8) – Fundsnet Services Online provides nonprofit organizations and colleges and universities with information on financial resources available on the Internet. There's a little bit of everything for everyone listed on this Web site. The site has links for dozens of project categories and organizations.

FIG. 9-8

©2006, Fundsnet Services Online. Reprinted with permission.

I clicked on the link for **Animal and Wildlife Grants** and links to a dozen grantmakers were listed.

Additional Private and Public Sector Grantmaker Websites

Environmental Grantmakers Association
http://www.ega.org/funders/funder.
  php?op=list

U.S. Agency International Development
http://www.usaid.gov/

Corporation for National and Community
  Service
http://www.nationalservice.org/

U.S. Department of Agriculture
http://www.usda.gov/wps/portal/usdahome

U.S. Department of Commerce
http://www.commerce.gov/

U.S. Department of Defense
http://www.defense.gov/

U.S. Department of Education
http://www.ed.gov/index.jhtml

U.S. Department of Energy
http://www.doe.gov/

U.S. Department of Health and Human
  Services
http://www.hhs.gov/

U.S. Department of Homeland Security
http://www.dhs.gov/dhspublic/

U.S. Department of Housing and Urban
  Development
http://www.hud.gov/

U.S. Department of the Interior
http://www.doi.gov/

U.S. Department of Justice
http://www.usdoj.gov/

U.S. Department of Labor
http://www.dol.gov/

U.S. Department of State
http://www.state.gov/

U.S. Department of Transportation
http://www.dot.gov/

U.S. Department of Treasury
http://www.ustreas.gov/

U.S. Department of Veteran Affairs
http://www.va.gov/

U.S. Environmental Protection Agency
http://www.epa.gov/

Institute of Museum and Library Services
http://www.imls.gov/

National Aeronautics and Space
  Administration
http://www.nasa.gov/externalflash/sts-121_
  front/index.html

U.S. National Archives and Records
  Administration
http://www.archives.gov/

National Endowment for the Arts
http://www.nea.gov/

National Endowment for the Humanities
http://www.neh.gov/

National Science Foundation
http://www.nsf.gov/

U.S. Small Business Administration
http://www.sba.gov/

U.S. Social Security Administration
http://www.ssa.gov/

For all of the 26 federal grantmaking agencies, the URLs listed above are for their home Web page. Their current grant funding announcements will always be posted on Grants.gov. I encourage you to visit each Web site to look for specific grant program information and the list of previous grantees for each program.

Index

C

D

©Thompson Publishing Group

©Thompson Publishing Group

H

hiring grant writing consultants, 25

Housing and Urban Development (HUD), U.S. Department of, 78–79

I

individuals as grantees, federal form for, 127–128

IRS consent form, CCR registration process, 42–43

K

Kellogg, W. K., Foundation, 56, 68, 69–70

key personnel, responsibility profiles for, 57

L

lobbying certification, 14–16, 105

Logic model tables, 56

looking for grants. *See* resources for grantseekers; searching for grants

M

management costs, 21–22

management plan, 57, 94

mandatory data form, federal grants, 119–123

meetings with funding agencies, 21

Minnesota common grant application form, 130–135

N

NAICS (North American Industry Classification System Code), 39

need, statement of, 56, 103

Neighborhood Networks Center, 78–79

North American Industry Classification System Code (NAICS), 39

O

online federal grants process, 3–4, 29–54

   applying for grants online, 51–54

   Grants.gov portal, 29

   registration, 30–47

      CCR registration, 35–44

      checklist, 30, 31–32

      completion of, 45–47

      credential provider, registration with, 43–44

      DUNS number, 33–35

   searching for grants online, 47–51

operating foundations, private, 66

P

pass-through foundations, 66

peer review of federal grants, 85–88

©Thompson Publishing Group

©Thompson Publishing Group

Practical, Time-Tested Guidance
For Grant Professionals

NEW! Federal Education Grants Management: What Administrators Need to Know

Federal Education Grants Management: What Administrators Need to Know is the only resource that focuses specifically on the unique compliance requirements associated with grants from the U.S. Department of Education. *You'll find:* A clear explanation – finally – of the Education Department's General Administrative Regulations and what they mean to you; How to find out which expenditures are allowable under federal grants; The ins-and-outs of key requirements like supplement-not-supplant and maintenance of effort; How to use the A-133 Single Audit Compliance Supplement to pinpoint the government's current audit priorities and avoid audit traps; Why understanding indirect costs can save you thousands of dollars; How to make sure your internal controls pass the government's tough tests; Understand the timeline for obligating funds and make sure you use every nickel by the deadline, and much more!

Federal Grants Management Handbook

The Federal Grants Management Handbook is the most comprehensive and trusted source for administering federal program funds – from submitting grant proposals to setting up financial management systems for payment and reporting… initiating audits and grant closeout to searching for best practices and procedures. Also available online.

Single Audit Information Service

The Single Audit Information Service is a comprehensive guide to all of the steps federal grantees and auditors must follow to ensure Single Audit Act compliance. From soliciting bids for audit services to preparing audit reports to resolving audit findings with federal officials, the Service provides detailed analyses of every aspect of single audit law and policy. It provides cost-effective and practical guidance on preparing for and performing single audits. All of the primary source documents grantees and auditors need are included – OMB circulars, GAO standards and federal agency regulations and guidance. Throughout the Service, you'll find helpful compliance tools such as checklists, sample reports and proven methods of single audit compliance. Regular Service updates provide up-to-date news and analysis.

NEW! Winning Strategies for Developing Grant Proposals – 2nd Edition

Winning Strategies for Developing Grant Proposals is a comprehensive, yet easy-to-read guide to writing effective grant proposals, and is written by a leading expert in the field. It includes the latest techniques and strategies for getting proposals funded.

Local/State Funding Report

Since 1972, Local/State Funding Report has detailed the latest federal funding programs, offering must-have intelligence and concise, comprehensive coverage of available dollars in rural development… healthcare… law enforcement… housing… juvenile justice… energy… emergency and disaster aid… transportation… the list goes on.

Guide to Federal Funding for Governments and Nonprofits

The Guide to Federal Funding for Government and Nonprofits offers fast, easy access to current, precise funding information on more than 750 federal grant-making programs – all grouped by function, not by agency. Thousands of your colleagues in local governments and in nonprofit agencies use the Guide to discover federal grant money every day for transportation… housing… social services… energy conservation… economic development… and much more.

Techniques for Monitoring Federal Subawards

This 119-page softbound book, written by the editors of the Federal Grants Management Handbook and Single Audit Information Service, explains grantees' and subrecipients' responsibilities, how to structure subaward agreements – and what provisions to include in those agreements, how to determine the most cost-effective monitoring methods, and details what auditors will look for in grantees' monitoring activities. Techniques include sample subaward agreements, checklists and excerpts from Office of Management and Budget circulars.

To start your subscription:
■ call toll-free: 1-800-677-3789 ■ order online at: www.thompson.com